Service Oriented Architecture

SOA — AN IMPLEMENTOR'S GUIDE

GETTING IT RIGHT

Contributing Authors:
....

David Besemer
Paul Butterworth
Luc Clément
Jim Green
Hemant Ramachandra
Jeff Schneider
Hub Vandervoort

Editor:
....

Jim Green

An Implementor's Guide to Service Oriented Architecture Getting It Right

www.SOAguidebook.com

ISBN-13: 978-0-9799304-0-9
ISBN-10: 0-9799304-0-5

First Edition
Printed April 2008

Printed and designed by Westminster Promotions.

TABLE OF CONTENTS

CHAPTER 1

Getting It Right

Jim Green
Chairman and CEO
Composite Software

1.1 Purpose Of The Book

The title of this book includes the word 'implementors'. That single word describes the focus of our work here. This book is a treatment of the practical issues an implementor would face when implementing a SOA. There are other very fine books on standards and basic education about SOA and web services. In fact, if you are not familiar with the web service standards, you might find some of this other material very useful as preparatory reading prior to digging into the implementation issues described herein.

It has frequently been observed that you can have an understanding of the philosophy of a SOA and the specifics of web service standards and still not know how to implement a SOA system that will provide lasting value to your enterprise. This book is an expedition through the considerations above the standards that come from practical experience in implementing a SOA. It is a practical book for the practitioner. The goal is to make the implementation of a SOA simpler and to encourage more people to deploy their own SOA. After all, today a SOA is considered the best way to create an integrated system that implements a consistent architecture on a large scale, providing flexibility and agility across applications and data for long lasting value.

As with other complex topics, those who have the right background, work on the issues daily, and study the topic in depth, will achieve an understanding more comprehensive than others. There are a handful of true experts in the industry that have achieved insights over time from their singular focus on the topics at hand. A main purpose of this book is to capture hard gained knowledge and make it available to a wide audience. Leveraging this expertise, in a way that we can all benefit from, has from the beginning been the primary goal of our endeavors. Hopefully we have achieved our goal.

> **KEY RECOMMENDATIONS:**
>
> - Don't let anyone overwhelm you by trying to teach you everything at once.
>
> - Do as much as you can digest, learn from it, and then add to it.
>
> - Regardless of the distance you travel, have confidence that you are on the right path.
>
> - SOA is the only good alternative for building large scale systems.

1.2 How We Put The Book Together

Since the SOA agenda covers a variety of different topics, no single person is authoritative across this wide spectrum. The approach, therefore, was to maximize the contributions of the book by leveraging the experience of different experts in each specific topic. Also, we went beyond those who create the basic standards and assembled a group of writers who understand the standards, the theory behind the leading technologies and products, and the issues with implementations. As a result, the book is stronger than if any one person were to author it.

Given the importance of the writers and their busy schedules, we did not attempt a group writing effort. Instead, we put together a 'compendium' of information, with each chapter standing alone. As such, there are minor differences of opinion that can be found in the book. Hopefully, this makes the book richer, and doesn't introduce confusion. You will find that in many areas there is no absolute answer to the questions. The different perspectives and focuses contained within are very much in alignment, but on some topics we felt that the reader is better served by exposure to differing points of view. In the final analysis, the more complex the issue, the more the reader will have to interpret and adapt the input here to their specific situation. There is no such thing as an 'SOA cookbook'.

1.3 How To Study The Book

Each chapter deals with a major topic that is important to your SOA implementation. Some effort has been expended to introduce topics in the general order that you need to understand them. However, each chapter is independent, so you can use the book as a general reference, and read each chapter as your interest turns to that topic. Therefore, the book is not a novel with a continuous story line that runs between the chapters. It is more of a reference guide. The many recommendations in the book are put forward for your consideration.

Much more is learned by actually 'doing' than by reading books (including this one). One of our biggest challenges therefore was to keep the book short. There's a lot more that could be said. But practicality was a top goal, so brevity was prioritized. In fact, even if you don't read the book, take a look at the key recommendations on the first page of each chapter, which are also summarized in the conclusion. Every attempt has been made to get to the most important points as soon as possible.

The contents of this book are the result of years of experience by experts. To achieve the goal of being succinct, much of the background has been omitted. As you gain your own experience with SOAs you will better understand the recommendations herein. It is hoped that this book can be a frequent reference, as well as an initial tutorial.

1.4 A Few Comments On SOAs

A SOA creates a flexible architecture, which allows for 'reconfiguring' over time. In fact, 'agility' has been identified as the largest single driver for a SOA. This attribute has more value when the target is a larger system that may change (following the simple assumption that larger systems are more difficult to modify than smaller ones). As you become more comfortable with a SOA approach you will find that this style of computing is not targeted toward being a better 'application architecture', but is more of an 'IT system architecture'. This perspective is important to understand as the reader moves through the material in the book.

As with all systems that are partitioned with strongly defined interfaces, SOA doesn't necessarily create the highest performing system. Just as assembly code can produce a faster application than a higher level language (at the cost of higher maintenance), breaking the principles of a SOA can increase performance. With the ever increasing performance of processors and networks, a SOA approach assumes that the business benefits of lower maintenance and increased flexibility are more than offset any inefficiencies by the use of standards, components, and modularity. This, however, may not be universally true. Web services standards may not be the correct approach for all situations, including very high performant applications. (This is the first example of practical advice in this book.)

However, in large scale systems, such as an enterprise IT architecture, there is no attractive alternative. Avoiding 'spaghetti code' at this level can not only result in reduced costs during development due to reuse, increased compatibility between heterogeneous systems due to the use of standards, lower maintenance costs due to a well structured architecture, but most importantly, it can retain an organization's ability to change as needed, and respond to changing business conditions. It is well worth the effort, and that's why we created this book—to help.

1.5 The Organization Of The Book

Chapter 2: Designing Services

Services are the fundamental building blocks of a SOA. The business functionality and the corporate data are contained within the services themselves. It is fairly straightforward to create a service, but also very possible to follow all of the standards the industry has worked so hard to create, yet not achieve the philosophy of a SOA and the benefits of reuse.

It is important to realize that web services standards (like SOAP, WSDL, HTTP, XML, UDDI, etc.) are specific and rigorously documented. SOA, on the other hand, is a methodology. Use of the standards while not adhering to the principles of the SOA 'philosophy' yields very little. Much of this issue is dealt with in the design of the individual service interfaces.

As indicated above, there are a number of implementation issues 'above' the standards. In this chapter, several of these are discussed, including topics like designing for reuse and error handling. You may or may not elect to follow the recommendations, but the issues discussed are important and should receive careful attention.

If you are an application developer or a service author, this is the most important chapter for you.

Chapter 3: Registries and Repositories

As your enterprise creates more services than can easily be remembered, you will need to put something in place to keep them organized. The industry standard for this is called UDDI. A UDDI registry has become a required part of all large scale SOA systems and serves as the 'SOA System of Record'.

Beyond the basics of providing the authoritative record of the service definitions, revisions, and description, the service registry has over time taken on an additional responsibility. The registry can make a major contribution toward the governance of the services through their lifecycle. Topics such as visibility (how does one discover a service), trust (what is the SLA for a service), and control (how does the organization control change) are discussed, along with numerous recommendations.

If you are a development manager and will be leveraging the 'reuse' capabilities of SOA, this chapter is required reading for you.

Chapter 4: Enterprise Service Buses

The simplest communication protocol for SOA is HTTP. However the request/reply model of this Internet protocol does not address all of the communication patterns that are of interest. Upgrading from the simple HTTP protocol to a richer infrastructure represented by an enterprise service bus (ESB) can add richness to your system. One example is the ability to implement publish/subscribe protocol capabilities.

An ESB is all about instantiating some mediation between the participants in the system. Once this is done, the mediating ESB can add value in a variety of ways, including protocol conversion, observation of system-wide performance, data transformation between systems, and intelligent routing.

The capabilities listed above are indeed impressive. However, the addition of an ESB also adds complexity, and numerous implementation trade-offs will be required. In addition, there are different 'types' of ESBs, and it is important to understand as much as possible prior to product selection and implementation.

If you are responsible for establishing the infrastructure for your SOA that will support all of the services this chapter is a must read.

Chapter 5: Runtime Management

Even with the right organization (Chapter 6), who are well trained (Chapter 7), well designed services (Chapter 2), the right infrastructure (Chapter 4), the right development practices and system of record (Chapter 3), things can/will still go wrong. In fact, if you do things well, you will create a system that is too sophisticated for you to easily observe it. To achieve the desired business objectives, the system must be appropriately monitored and governed at runtime.

This aspect of a SOA is fascinating in that the better things work, the less you see. After achieving success with automation and transparency, you then need to institute observe-ability to provide the proper runtime governance, trouble-shooting, and control. Issues include practical topics such as understanding what the current topology is and what is happening, assessing the current health of the overall system, and ensuring the continuing integrity of the system as it evolves—in other words, keeping it running and under control.

If you are responsible for the overall SOA system design, you must incorporate management into your plans. If you are responsible for the operation of the SOA system this is your most important chapter.

Chapter 6: Organizing For Success

As you move from large applications to modular components, there are more interactions between the software components, and between the providers and consumers of the components. Assuming that components are smaller than applications, there will be more of them. And assuming that different components/services will be created by different people, then there is an organizational impact generated by a SOA.

Many times, the communication required to work things out actually improves design and avoids problems later. Contrary to what some say, your existing personnel are probably fine, but they may need to think differently, assume somewhat different roles, and learn a little, but they can do this.

If you're an organization manager and only read one chapter, this is the one.

Chapter 7: Capability Development

The system you build will be a reflection of the skill and dedication of the people who put it together. One of the first steps, then, is to prepare and educate your team. When approaching a SOA project proper training cannot be overemphasized.

It is critical to understand that you should not view SOA as the objective. The objective is to build a system that supports your organizational goals. SOA is only an 'approach' to putting that system in place. From this perspective, it is clear that the system should be put together by those who know your business best. It will be easier to train your own staff (who know your business) on SOAs than to train outside SOA experts on your business.

If you are charged with the creation of the SOA implementation team this chapter is required reading for you.

Chapter 8: Pulling IT Together

SOA provides value when it is implemented, regardless of the scope. So it is important to get started on the journey, regardless of where you start. Measuring progress is important as success begets more success, and failure begets improvement. Leveraging the hard earned knowledge of experts will help you accelerate your journey. So use the recommendations as your implementor's guide.

If your mission is to drive successful SOA implementations, you will want to leverage the key recommendations summarized in this chapter.

1.6 What's Not In The Book

A book such as this needs to be tightly focused and not too long. As such, there are topics that are beyond the reach of our efforts here. We have oriented our writing toward those that are starting their SOA efforts to help them overcome the initial learning curve. There is not enough space to deal with several of the advanced topics. If you move beyond the level of this book and become frustrated by its incompleteness, while frustrating to you, it would signify success of a sort for the authors. Should you find yourself in such a state, you now know where to find us to get more help.

As you build your SOA system, it will enable and support a wide variety of uses and application types. As tempting as it is, we have avoided expanding into the 'application arena'. You may, for example, be interested in providing readable information to users through portals, collating and calculating information in a business intelligence (BI) report, propagating and synchronizing information between systems through application integration (EAI), or automating a set of business tasks through business process management (BPM). All of these areas (and others) will find your SOA infrastructure enormously enabling. Unfortunately, dealing with these topics alone would constitute a complete book in its own right. We have therefore had to set aside these topics for another time and place.

Despite its limitations, this book not only provides a significant amount of factual information, but conveys principals and methodology. If you maintain the discipline described herein, you can go far beyond what we have written and create your own chapters as extensions to ours.

1.7 Conclusion

No one thinks it all through at once. No one puts all of the pieces in place perfectly. But once on the right path, it is more straightforward than it first seems, and additional pieces fall into place logically. Don't let anyone overwhelm you by trying to teach you everything at once. Do as much as you can digest, learn from it, and then add to it. Regardless of the distance you travel, you will have accomplished a lot. Mostly though, you will have instantiated a system that others can extend. The days of calcified IT systems are numbered.

Whether you are planning a major overhaul of your large scale IT system, or you want to create a few services using the new standards, a couple of hours of study and preparation may help avoid common pitfalls and propel you toward success. If so, then our efforts here will be rewarded.

Good luck with your endeavors.

CHAPTER 2

Designing Services

David Besemer
Chief Technology Officer
Composite Software

2.1 Services Introduction

In a service oriented architecture, *services* provide the basis for communications between systems and technologies. Services are well-defined units of functionality that are accessible over the network via standard protocols. They are invoked by software, and are not accessed by a human user. In other words, services are more like a remote procedure calls. The system that implements a service is called a *provider*, while the system that uses the service is called a *consumer*.

Services can be built in a variety of ways, but standards and guidelines exist to promote interoperability and reuse in an enterprise-class service oriented architecture. The central standards relevant to service implementation and deployment are *XML, SOAP, WSDL, and UDDI (refer to the following illustration),* and services that conform to these standards are called *web services*. A web service is actually a collection of individual service operations, each of which can be thought of as an individual procedure.

KEY RECOMMENDATIONS:

- Base your services on vendor independent industry standards to ensure the best reuse and interoperability.

- Create and deploy your services in an appropriate and best-of-breed infrastructure to ensure operational efficiencies (e.g. an *information server* for data services; an *application server* for transaction services.)

- Design service interfaces that are simple, consistent, well-documented, and motivated by business requirements to ensure adoption, reusability, and expandability.

- Employ security policies to meet the business needs of your enterprise.

Figure 2.1: Service Invocation

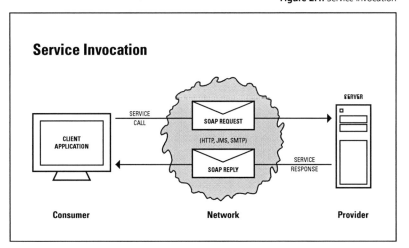

DESIGNING SERVICES

INDIVIDUAL SERVICE OPERATION

An individual service operation is invoked using a SOAP call, which encapsulates the service request message (and subsequently, a response message) for transport over the network – you can think of it as the envelope that contains a letter. The SOAP call can be transported between consumer and provider over a variety of mechanisms such as HTTP, SMTP, or a message bus. Because of the wide availability of HTTP infrastructures within enterprises, most web service calls today are transported via HTTP. Recently, however, the use of message buses (ESBs) has been increasing for transporting web service calls.

SERVICE REQUEST AND MESSAGES

The service request and response messages themselves are written in XML. The SOAP standard defines two possible XML message formats, RPC and document, and two encodings, SOAP and literal. Most experts agree that the best way to ensure interoperability is to use the document format with literal encoding.

WEB SERVICE SPECIFICATION LANGUAGE DOCUMENT

The complete specification of a web service (i.e., the location of the service on the network, the specific operations available, and the request and response message formats, etc.) is embodied in a WSDL document, which service consumers consult to figure out how to use the service. The WSDL can be considered the API definition for a web service, and as such, it defines the contract between provider and consumer.

UDDI DIRECTORY

WSDLs are often catalogued in a UDDI directory that consumers consult to discover services and their providers.

Unfortunately standards alone are not enough to ensure service interoperability. Additional guidelines have been created by an organization called the *Web Services Interoperability Organization* (WS-I). WS-I's *Basic Profile* defines best practices within the Web service standards and promotes the highest possibility for reuse and platform independence. Organizations can benefit greatly from following recommendations of the WS-I Basic Profile for their service development and deployment.

Services generally either provide data to the consumer, or they create or modify data in an underlying system. The former are called data services, and the later are called *transaction services*. An example of a data service might be *retrieveOrdersForCustomer*, which might take a customer number as an input parameter. An example of a transaction service might be *updateOrderShippingStatus*, which might take an order number and the updated shipping status as input parameters. These services present separate challenges to the service provider and they are generally created and deployed using different infrastructures. Data services are created and deployed in an *information server,* while transaction services are created and deployed in an *application server*. These different types of services and their associated infrastructures are described in detail later in this chapter.

Getting started with service development and deployment in your enterprise does not have to be difficult or expensive. Rather than following a 'boil the ocean' approach that seeks to define all enterprise-wide services needs in advance, it is commonly recommended to take an incremental, organic approach to service development and deployment. Choose a project that will benefit from a service-oriented approach and begin creating a collection of services needed for that specific project. Once the first project is in production, select another project can reuse some of the services from the first project. You will more than likely need to create new services for your second project, but you will probably be able to reuse one or more of the services created for the first project. When reusing services, you may discover that the services you created for the first project require modification or augmentation to facilitate reuse, which is perfectly normal. Because the collection of consumers is limited at this point, you will usually be able to modify them with little effort. More important, you will have learned what it takes to create reusable and scalable services for your enterprise. This pragmatic, incremental methodology allows you to show value quickly and to refine your strategy as your service usage grows.

Securing service calls can be a complex topic, but the good news is that there are relatively straightforward approaches to security that can be implemented easily. As with services standards, there are both standards and best practices that can be combined to prescribe an approach that we will explore later in this chapter.

2.2 Data Services

An estimated two thirds of all services will be data services, making them the most prevalent form of services in an enterprise. Data services provide data to a consumer in a form that addresses current and ongoing business demands. The focus of data services is to make it easy for consumers to access and use enterprise data in support of their business processes. However, in many cases this requested form of the data does not match how the data is stored in legacy systems, so the data must be transformed, aggregated, combined, or otherwise modified to support current business needs. This is the primary role of a data service: To virtualize (abstract) data from its native form for use (and reuse) in the modern enterprise, while hiding (encapsulating) the complex work of getting the data into a form for consumption. However, providing data to a service consumer in an appropriate form can be challenging for a variety of reasons, including:

- Data required to satisfy demand may be distributed amongst two or more systems. For example, the bulk of information about an order might be stored in the ERP system (e.g., SAP), but customer interactions regarding the order might be stored in a CRM system (e.g., SalesForce.com).

- Protocols for getting data out of the underlying systems are vendor specific and highly varied. You may be able to retrieve customer data directly from your customer master using SQL, but you might have to use a web service call—or worse—a vendor-specific API to get the order information from the ERP system.

- The format of the data from the underlying systems is probably not XML, and as a result, will require transformation prior to supporting a web service call. The native format possibilities for the underlying data are numerous (e.g. relational, delimited, proprietary, hierarchical, etc.) and manually mapping these to XML is not practical.

- Legacy semantics of the data will not necessarily match current use cases. For example, prior to the dot-com era, an internal data source might have been created to hold information about a customer. At that time, it was reasonable to establish fields regarding 'marketing opportunities', In the current usage, however, that same data might be presented to a customer in a self-service portal as 'privacy preferences'.

- Approximately ten percent of enterprise data is replicated in data warehouses and data marts, while the remaining ninety percent is in operational systems. It is important to maintain high levels of performance in these operational systems. Data services need to optimize data access performance as well as utilize intelligent caching and other advanced techniques.

2.2.1 Data Services Levels

Transforming data from its native 'physical' environment to its required 'virtual' form can comprise a complex and difficult set of operations. One recommended approach to address these data transformation challenges is to break the problem into smaller pieces (see Figure 2.2), which manifests itself as layered services of varied granularity, including:

- **Physical Services.** Physical services lie just above the data source and they transform the data into a form that is easily consumed by higher-level services. For a well-designed database, these services may be unnecessary because the data can be understood and used as is. However, many packaged applications store their data in a form that is designed for optimal use within that application, and that form of the data does not lend itself well to direct and transparent access. For this kind of data, it is very useful to layer a collection of light transformation services just above the physical layer. These services can change element names, cast data types, and augment record contents. The output of these services can still be considered relatively raw, physical data, but it has been put into a form that is cleaner and more useful.

- **Business Services.** Business services embody the bulk of the transformation logic that converts data from its physical form into its required business form. These services should be thought of as a provider of the canonical data representations for your business (e.g., customer, supplier, product, order, shipment, etc.). There may be several 'layers' of business services—especially if intermediate transformations are useful as business services in their own right. For example, if your company sells cellular and residential phone service, you may have a 'customer' business service, and above it you might also have a 'cellularCustomer' business service (which leverages but refines the 'customer' service). Business services can be seen as providing master data and transaction data to the rest of your processes.

- **Application Services.** Application services leverage business services to provide data optimally to the consuming applications. Application services are lightweight wrappers that match the business services with their actual usage in the application layer. If the application layer is a modern BPM environment, no transformation may be necessary – that is, it may be possible to use the business services directly via SOAP invocations. On the other hand, if the application layer is a business intelligence platform, it probably needs to access the data as if it were stored in a database. So an application service that looks like a virtual database table will be necessary. As application services are created and used, discipline should be applied to avoid business logic creeping into this layer. If data is transformed with business logic, that logic should reside in the business services layer.

The elimination of duplicated enterprise data and increased opportunities for reuse are the main advantages of establishing logical layers within the pool

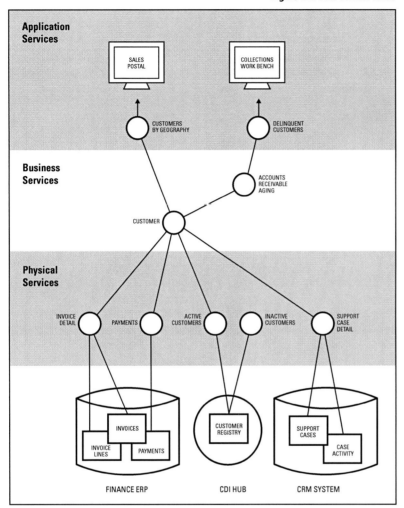

of data services. With these logical levels of service granularity in use, you will find that the business services can be reused throughout the enterprise with few additional transformations required.

2.2.2 Data Services Infrastructure

The challenges associated with providing data services, beyond the usual scalability and high-availability production needs, dictate the need for an environment designed specifically to easily create, deploy, and maintain data services. This infrastructure environment is called an 'information server' and several vendors offer products in this category. An information server is distinctly different from an application server (which will be discussed in the

Data Services Information Server	Transaction Services Application Server
Key Features	
Container for Data Services	Container for Transaction Services
Data Access Standards	J2EE Standards
Data Federation	Session Management
Data Retrieval Performance	Memory/Thread Management
Data Transformation	Concurrency
Data Caching	Security
Data Security	

next section on transaction services). Most mature SOA infrastructures will have both an information server and an application server. (see Figure 2.3)

When selecting information server infrastructure software on which to build your data services layer, there are many things to consider, including:

• **Adherence to Standards.** The key tenets of a service oriented architecture are loose coupling and reusability. It is impossible to achieve either of these if your services do not conform to standards and best practices.

• **Performance and Scalability.** The run-time execution of individual data services must be intelligent and efficient, and the overall infrastructure must provide massive scalability. Advanced query planning and optimization are the keys to intelligent execution – it's not enough to simply throw more processing power at the problem.

• **Ease-of-Use.** One reason to use an infrastructure that focuses specifically on data services is to eliminate work that would otherwise be done elsewhere. If the environment is not easy for developers to use and maintain, adoption will be slow and efficiencies will be lost.

• **Data Caching.** In addition to being a virtualization layer, the data services infrastructure is also an insulation/buffering layer. This cannot be effectively accomplished without providing a caching mechanism. There should be both implicit and explicit caching opportunities, and it should be possible to cache both query results and procedure calls.

• **Access to Data Sources.** An enterprise's data services layer must provide access to all structured enterprise data. This includes relational databases, third-party data services, packaged applications (e.g., SAP, Siebel), files (e.g., Excel), directories (e.g., LDAP), and legacy mainframes (e.g., VSAM). It should also provide the capability to expand its reach through custom development, allowing even the most obscure data source to participate in the data services layer.

- **Data Quality Management.** A significant amount of enterprise data is dirty and incomplete. Some of the messiness can be addressed with straightforward transformation capabilities, but some of it must be attacked with robust data cleansing functionality.

- **Strong and Flexible Security Mechanisms.** Exactly what your enterprise needs will be determined by your industry and business requirements, but the infrastructure software should provide general purpose mechanisms to implement a variety of security measures.

- **Vision and Focus.** The challenges associated with the data services infrastructure comprise a discipline that is unique. The vendor you choose to provide this capability to your enterprise should be clearly focused on this problem, and have a vision for advancing the state of the art. Several vendors claim data services functionality as part of their broad offerings, but that slice of the platform will never get the focus it needs to be effective. We recommend that you select a vendor that offers best-of-breed in data services technology.

2.2.3 Enterprise-wide Data Services Layer

As the collection of reusable data services in your enterprise grows and the production requirements of the service consumers become more demanding, the information server will expand to form an enterprise-wide data services layer. This clustered and highly available infrastructure establishes a virtualization layer between enterprise systems that store data and enterprise applications that use data. The presence of this data services layer in an enterprise provides several long-term benefits, including:

- Consumers of a particular type of data will get that data from the same shared service, ensuring consistency of data across the enterprise.

- New business application requirements are less daunting since the IT organization can now provide the application developer with the exact data they need to be most effective—regardless of how the data exists in the underlying systems. This sort of data access agility is unheard of in today's enterprise IT environment.

- Data consumers will be decoupled from the underlying physical systems, allowing legacy systems to be changed, migrated, or retired without affecting the consuming applications. Only the data services layer will need to be modified to accommodate the underlying physical changes.

- As data capacity requirements grow, the data services layer can be scaled to accommodate increasing demand. And because caching is available in this layer, it may not be necessary to add corresponding capacity to the underlying physical data source.

- System consolidation will require data to be grafted from only one of the affected systems into the data services layer without affecting the high-level business applications. This efficiency overcomes the consolidation chaos commonly resulting from mergers and acquisitions.

2.3 Transaction Services

Transaction services implement individual business operations that are executed as part of a larger business process. The effect of invoking a transaction service is the creation or modification of data in an underlying data repository. The logic encapsulated in a transaction service represents your enterprise's definition of what it means to, for example, create a customer or update an inventory level.

Some transaction services will be provided inherently as part of a packaged application (e.g., SAP), and a user indirectly invokes them when a user employs the application's user interface. Although many packaged application vendors do not yet provide their functionality as standard services for use outside their user interface, most are moving in this direction.

Other transaction services will need to be developed to implement specific, unique business logic. These services are generally built by IT developers in a software development environment like an application server (e.g., IBM WebSphere). These environments offer powerful development tools and efficient deployment environments. They also provide standard security and transaction frameworks.

Transaction services generally modify data in a single underlying data source, and they are therefore generally connected directly to that data source (rather than relying on the data services layer as an abstraction). This tight coupling is acceptable because a collection of transaction services normally 'owns' the data source it is modifying. However, transaction services also often need access to data to carry out their business logic. For this data they should invoke the same data services that everybody else uses (through the data services infrastructure).

As the names imply, transaction services implement the logical equivalent of a business transaction (e.g., place an order). As such, an important characteristic of a transaction service is that it either completely succeeds or completely fails, leaving no artifacts or incorrect data behind. This is not difficult if the transaction service is modifying a single relational database that implements transaction semantics, but it can be more challenging if it is working with a set of underlying (finer grained) transaction services that are inherently stateless, or if its transaction data is split among more than one data source. The application server environment usually provides strong transactional models that will assist the developer with this challenge, but the developer needs to use them.

Just as important as the transactional integrity of the service, it is critical to define the scope of the service at the appropriate granularity: Your transaction services should provide business-level granularity so the consumer is not required to think about the interplay between fine-grained physical data components. For example, if you wanted to provide a service for updating the on-hand inventory level for a product, the service should simply take the increment or decrement amount as input, and then internally handle the possibilities for concurrency. As another example, if you wanted to provide a service that deletes a customer, the service should also delete the customer's associated orders, payments, service calls, etc. In other words, the consumer of the service should not have to know the business rules associated with deleting a customer; the service should simply encapsulate the rules and offer the comprehensive service to the consumer.

A transaction is not a substitute for application integration which would be accomplished with an ESB layer or a similar system with traditional EAI capability. That is, it should not be the responsibility of the transaction service to update the same data in multiple underlying sources. The transaction service should modify its system(s) of record only. Any required propagation of new or modified data to other systems should be done after the transaction is completed, and it should be performed by an appropriate infrastructure that is designed for this kind of pattern.

2.3.1 Transaction Services Infrastructure

Important considerations when choosing a transaction server development environment are a superset of the those when choosing an application server environment. In most cases, an enterprise will already have at least one in-house application server environment which IT is familiar with, and that same environment can probably be effectively used to create and deploy transaction services. Since application servers are well understood by most IT departments, the following list comprises only additional considerations that should influence the selection of an application server for building transaction services.

- **Service Standards Support.** The transaction environment should offer built-in support for XML manipulation, SOAP semantics, and automatic WSDL creation. In addition, it should be easy to implement services that conform to the WS-I Basic Profile for web services.

- **Vendor Neutrality.** Make sure the services that are created in the environment do not require software from the same vendor on the consumer side of the interaction. This is a key point in guaranteeing truly reusable and loosely coupled services.

- **Robust Transaction Semantics.** The environment should support various transaction implementation models, from two-phase commit to compensation models, and it should be easy for the software developer to wrap his work in a reliable transaction scope.

- **Easy and Efficient Service Invocation.** Transaction service developers will need to access data from the data services infrastructure, so it is important that service invocation be easy and efficient for the developer to accomplish. Otherwise, the developer will be tempted to access data directly, thereby compromising the abstraction provided by the data services layer.

- **Strong and Flexible Security Mechanisms.** Exactly what your enterprise needs will be determined by your requirements, but the software vendor should provide general purpose mechanisms to implement a variety of security measures. Later in this chapter there is a section that describes service security.

2.4 Service Interface Design

The web service standards and recommendations leave service creators with broad latitude for designing service interfaces. From one viewpoint, this is a very positive situation: You can design service interfaces that exactly meet the needs of your enterprise. From another viewpoint, however, this broad latitude creates a problem because it will be easy to inadvertently create service interfaces that have no relationship with one another, are difficult to use, and the resulting services will embody no unified design vision. In other words, it will be a mess.

You may be able to take service design guidance from the dominant packaged application vendor in your enterprise. Some of the application vendors have made significant progress in providing service-based APIs. SAP currently provides the most complete treatment, although it requires their installed base to upgrade to take full advantage of their offering. Other vendors have not made significant public commitments to service-based APIs, so it's not clear what direction they will take. If you are a customer of one of these vendors you should demand to see their plans so that you can begin your own planning. When you learn more about the APIs that your vendors provide, you can consider modeling your own APIs along the same lines, or wrap those APIs in your own to extend or elevate their interfaces. The guidelines below will help you determine whether the vendor-provided APIs are appropriate for your needs.

You should think of your service interfaces as the public API into your enterprise data. As such, care should be taken to make them useful, easy to learn, well documented, consistent, supportable, and extendable. If you have ever been on the consumer side of a poorly designed API, you can appreciate the need for simplicity and elegance – it should all hang together and make sense to the consumer.

Fortunately, we can learn something about how to do this from another software development paradigm: Object oriented programming. In this paradigm, a developer creates a class for a specific type of data, and the class implements methods (procedures) for manipulating that data. Related classes that work with each other to accomplish something broader are usually grouped into packages, and multiple packages that form a comprehensive framework are packaged and distributed together.

An analogous paradigm can be used as a guideline for developing your services.

- **Categorize Your Data.** Design a collection of services for manipulating a particular category of data. For example, *customer*. Services should be provided for creating, updating, deleting, and retrieving customers. There may be several services for each of these activities. For example, you might provide multiple ways to retrieve customers.

- **Group Services by Category.** Create these sets of services for each category of data in your enterprise. The categories of data will either be master data (e.g., employee, customer, and product) or operational data (e.g., order, PO, shipment). The collection of services might be slightly different for these two categories of data, but the differences should be motivated by requirements of your service consumers.

- **Judiciously Provide Cross-Category Services.** Where necessary, create services that operate on multiple categories of data, but leverage the service interfaces you designed for the individual data types. For example, you might need to provide a service that retrieves a customer and all of their orders. Make sure the input parameter to specify the customer matches the input parameter for specifying a customer in the collection of customer-specific services. Furthermore, make sure the schema of the returned data (customer and orders) match the schemas for customer and order data returned in the data-specific services.

- **Package Related Services Together.** Finally, group related services together in a single WSDL to provide consumers access to the whole framework at once.

The important thing is to avoid designing individual service interfaces in isolation. If consumers are familiar with your services for manipulating an employee, it should be natural and easy for them to begin using your services that manipulate a customer. It sounds like common sense, but it will make a huge difference in the adoption rate of your shared services.

2.4.1 Individual Service Design

With this service framework in mind, we can turn our attention to the design of the individual services, beginning with some guidelines, including:

- Keep interfaces as simple as possible. Service consumers do not want a comprehensive service that does everything possible on a particular kind of data, but requires an overly complex service call simply to, for example, change a phone number of a customer. Service consumers want it to be easy and obvious how to accomplish their task.

- A service that modifies data should either completely succeed or cleanly fail: Without leaving corrupted or incomplete data behind. Exactly how the service accomplishes this will depend on the implementation, but the consistency contract with the customer should not be compromised.

- Try not to provide services to consumers that would allow them to unwittingly do harm to enterprise data. For example, if you provide a service that sets the inventory level of a product, a service consumer could retrieve the existing inventory level, add some recently received product to the count, and then update the inventory to the new count. Unfortunately, if two different consumers perform this sequence at roughly the same time, it would be possible to lose inventory because one of the consumers can overwrite the other consumer's change. It is preferable to provide a service that increments or decrements inventory, and the service's implementation should employ a locking strategy to ensure correct and consistent behavior.

- Establish and use a standard error reporting scheme for all services (refer to the following section for more details).

2.4.2 Error Handling

Reporting errors that occur during service invocation should be done in a way that allows the client to handle errors in a consistent way. There are four kinds of errors that can occur during service invocation, including:

- **Communication Errors.** These happen when the service infrastructure is unavailable to complete the invocation (e.g., the network is down). These errors will usually manifest as something outside the SOAP standard (e.g., an HTTP connect error). As a service implementer, you don't have control over how to report them. You should, however, perform internal testing with your own infrastructure to see how errors will be reported to your consumers. This will enable you to provide direction for handling errors effectively in the service orchestration environment.

- **System Errors.** These occur inside the execution of the service, but they are related to the system rather than to the application logic. For example, temporary disk space for assembling results might become full, or a required data source is currently unavailable. These errors are usually not correctable by the caller. This class of errors should be reported to the caller as a *fault* in the SOAP invocation, with the standard fault code of *soap:Server*. SOAP faults are like exceptions, and they are returned to the caller instead of the return message. The caller can *catch* the SOAP fault and process it accordingly.

- **Application Errors.** These are errors in processing business logic that defines the service. For example, when a user attempts to set a phone number to an invalid string. Application errors should also be reported using SOAP faults, but with the standard fault code of *soap:Client,* which distinguishes them from system errors. It is useful to establish a convention for reporting additional information in the detail element of the fault. The WS-I Basic Profile for interoperability allows arbitrary sub-elements underneath the detail element so a schema snippet can be created and included in every SOAP fault. This will result in offering additional information that will be useful to the client (e.g., an application error code).

- **Application Warnings.** These are non-fatal errors that are discovered during the processing of the business logic. They are not severe enough to cause the request to fail, but you might like to tell the caller about them For example, there might be a service that updates a customer's address, and the service caller might provide a zip code that does not match the city and state in the address. While it may be reasonable to allow this service to succeed (your own business rules will determine this), it will be useful to issue a warning that the customer's address data is not internally consistent. If you plan to issue warnings with your services you should create a standard part of the document schema for reporting them. All return messages should include the warning component as an optional part of the return message. The caller can choose to ignore it, but the information is available if they want to process the error.

2.4.3 Example

With these guidelines in mind, designing specific service interfaces required for a type of data can be straightforward. Here is a typical set of services you might create.

- Design an XML representation (schema) for the data.
- Design CRUD (Create, Retrieve, Update, Delete) service operations for the data (leveraging the XML schema).
- Design supplemental services to further manipulate the data, as required by the business.

To make these service development activities clearer, let's apply them to an example of customer data:

- **Design a XML representation (schema) for the type of data that the services will work with.** A customer represented in XML might begin something like this:

```
<customer>
   <id>123456</id>
   <creationTimestamp>2007-01-13 14:35:22.345</
   <creationTimestamp>
   <modificationTimestamp>2007-02-09 08:30:55.127</
   <modificationTimestamp>
```

```
<firstName>John</firstName>
<lastName>Smith</lastName>
<gender>M</gender>
<birthDate>1962-07-10</birthDate>
...
</customer>
```

- **Create a service for creating a new customer.** The input document should be the schema designed above. The service should confirm that all required data elements have been provided. It is possible to specify required and optional elements in the XML schema, but different uses of the same schema will have different requirements, so it is better to embody this business logic in the service itself. The service should automatically create some of the fields for the consumer (e.g., the customer id should be uniquely generated, and the timestamps should be handled automatically). The service should return the complete customer (as created) using the same schema.

- **Create a service for easily modifying an existing customer.** The input document should be the customer schema designed above. The id element specifies which customer is to be updated and the other elements will be used to update (overwrite) the customer's data.

- **Provide a service for easily deleting a customer.** The input document for this service should simply contain the customer's id—no other data should be required. The service itself should implement all business logic required to delete a customer from the enterprise. For example, it may be desirable to remove a customer's orders, payments, and service calls as well. Whatever the business logic is, it should be performed in a manner that can guarantee integrity of the underlying data.

- **Provide a service for easily retrieving (querying) customers.** The input document should be the customer schema, and then only the provided fields will be used to match existing customers. For example, if an id is provided, a single customer will be matched. If a last name is provided, multiple customers may be matched. The service should return a list of customers that match the input values.

- **Provide additional services for retrieving customers in other useful ways, as dictated by the requirements of the consumers.** The input document should be designed to accommodate the necessary input data. The service should return a list of customers (using the same schema as all the other services). For example, somebody may want a service that retrieves all customers who placed orders since a given date (or between two dates).

- **Provide additional services for operating on customers, as dictated by the requirements of the consumers.** Again, the input document should be designed to accommodate the necessary input data. In this case, the output document should be designed to accommodate the service requirements. For example, somebody may want a service that counts customers by geography, returning a list of countries, states, or zip codes, and the corresponding customer count for each geography. The important thing about designing these services is to wait until they are needed. Designing these services in the absence of real business requirements is usually time wasted.

This methodology can be applied repeatedly to all the data in your enterprise. It is not recommended that you do it all at once, however, because when consumers begin to use services you have provided, you will learn lessons that can be applied to future efforts. Expanding your service collection incrementally, as needed by the consumer community, is the most efficient way to proceed.

2.5 Security Considerations

Security of enterprise data is always a priority, and introducing services as an access and manipulation paradigm adds new challenges. Since each enterprise has its own philosophies on security, the best approach to service security is to extend your enterprise's current security strategies to these new paradigms. In keeping with that idea, this section is not a service security cookbook, but is provided to help educate the readers about the available security alternatives.

There are three areas of security to be considered when deploying services:

• User Authentication
• Access Authorization
• Message Privacy

Several standards exist that contribute to service security implementation (HTTP Authorization, WS-Security, SSL, SAML, etc). However, as with other web services standards, there is quite a bit of latitude, and therefore broad variability, as to how security is actually implemented. The WS-I has formulated the *WS-I Basic Security Profile* in an attempt to narrow the range, and increase both security and interoperability, and we urge readers to consult this recommendation to assist with security questions.

2.5.1 User Authentication

Services are essentially executable modules, available to other consumers over the network. But who gets to execute them? It is possible to provide services that are open to anyone, but this is not the usual situation in an enterprise. Rather, access to a service usually requires a user to be identified and authenticated so that authorization can be performed. With web services, this can be done in a number of ways:

• **HTTP Basic Authentication.** If your services are accessed over HTTP, your server can use HTTP basic authentication to require a user to provide a username and password to essentially 'log in' to invoke the service. This is a simple but effective mechanism for authentication that is widely used. When combined with a wire-level encryption (i.e., SSL), it is quite secure. This kind of authentication mechanism is roughly equivalent to a normal client login to a database today.

- **SAML.** This is a standard XML-based authentication mechanism modeled on the presentation of a secured token. SAML is considered the future of web service authentication but it is not yet widely used. It is recommended that you use a service infrastructure provider that plans to support SAML within a year. The SAML model is similar to Kerberos, so if you currently use something similar to Kerberos for your enterprise authentication, you will be interested in learning about SAML for use with your service implementations.

- **Custom Login Service.** You can provide a custom service that accepts a user's login credentials and returns an identity token. The identity token is then presented as part of the input to each subsequent service invocation. This mechanism is widely used today, but it does not promote interoperability of services, and it requires all services to accommodate the mechanism. Combined with a wire-level encryption, however, it is quite secure. You can think of this approach as being equivalent to a login box on a web page portal where the web protocol is probably encrypted (HTTPS), but the actual authentication is processed by the application (which is probably running in an application server).

2.5.2 Access Authorization

Once a user is authenticated to the service infrastructure, there are two types of authorization to consider:

- Does the user have permission to invoke the service?
- Does the user have permission to access all of the data returned by the service?

The WS-I Basic Security Profile addresses both of these in detail, so we will not duplicate that effort in this book. However, some general considerations can be offered, including:

- Your service infrastructure should provide general purpose enforcement mechanisms for these. It should not be necessary to build authorization logic into the service implementation itself.

- If a user does not have permission to invoke a service, the simplest way to indicate this is to immediately return a SOAP fault.

- A service may return a rich XML document containing a significant amount of data, but the current user may be authorized to see only portion of the data. In this case, only the sections of the document for which the user is authorized will be populated. Again, your service infrastructure should provide general purpose enforcement mechanisms for this type of security.

2.5.3 Message Privacy

Services operate using request and response messages, the contents of which are generally XML documents. When transported over an unsecured network, these request and response messages are potentially vulnerable to snooping, which dictates the need for message privacy strategies. There are two main mechanisms used to accomplish this today, SSL for HTTP and WS-Security.

SSL for HTTP

Most services today are accessed via HTTP. SSL can be used to provide a secure (encrypted) point-to-point communication channel between the consumer and the provider (HTTPS). This is the same mechanism used by your web browser when you submit your credit card information during a purchase. The advantage of this mechanism is that it's easy to implement and easy to use. Most secure web service calls are protected by this mechanism today. There are, however, two main disadvantages of this privacy mechanism:

- **Proxy Protection.** If the service call goes through a proxy, the secure communications channel does not extend through the proxy, potentially leaving the communications vulnerable. It is not always clear to the provider or the consumer exactly where proxies exist in the call chain, so care should be taken.

- **In-transit Protection.** The encryption exists only on the point-to-point communication channel, and does not secure the message itself. If the SOA architecture includes mechanisms for service mediation (e.g., store-and-forward), the message is unprotected when not being transported. Similarly, if messages are logged to a disk or database, the message is not secured.

WS-Security

This is a collection of security standards designed to secure web services. Its scope is actually broader than transport privacy (it can also be used to assist with authentication), but it is primarily aligned with message security. The WS-Security standards are not currently in wide use, but it is expected that they will be as SOA implementations proliferate. A comprehensive discussion of WS-Security is beyond the scope of this chapter, but the following is a summary of what it provides:

- **Element-level Message Encryption**. Specific sections of a service message (i.e., the XML document) can be encrypted for privacy. This encryption is within the message, so it persists for the life of the message—regardless of how or where the message travels.

- **Message Integrity**. Allows the consumer of the message to reliably determine whether the message has been modified since being created.

- **Message Authentication**. Reliably identifies and guarantees the sender/creator of the message.

Your service infrastructure vendor should provide support for WS-Security—it should be an important part of your vendor selection criteria.

Security is a broad and deep topic, and we have only scratched the surface in this section. The important point is that you can extend your current enterprise security strategies to embrace services as well. We recommend you formulate your enterprise's service security requirements, and then work with the service infrastructure vendors to put software in place that meets those requirements.

2.6 Conclusion

The collection of services you create will form the foundation for your service oriented architecture efforts. Your foundation's strength and longevity will be enhanced if you follow the suggestions outlined in this chapter.

You can begin creating services today. You do not need to wait until you have a comprehensive set of requirements, and you can get started with limited staff and investment. Select a project with specific well-known needs, and build the services needed to address those requirements.

CHAPTER 3

Registries And Repositories

Luc Clément
Co-Chairman

**OASIS UDDI Specification
Technical Committee**

Service-oriented architectures (SOAs) enable IT to remain agile and deliver the capabilities to the business. However, this flexibility is typically created through an increased number of smaller reusable components interacting with each other rather than larger enterprise applications. This interaction creates interdependencies which can reduce reliability and uptime if not carefully managed. Understanding these interdependencies is required to ensure that the business services you create can be adapted when faced with a need to make a change.

Success depends on the ability to coordinate activities as business services are implemented and deployed. Application architects, functional analysts, project managers, and test and operations teams can be geographically or organizationally distributed, different services can be in varied states of their lifecycle at any given time, and the potential for confusion is high. Organizations therefore need effective management and controls to cope with the business services lifecycle.

As services multiply, the problem is compounded. An uncontrolled, broad adoption of a SOA can lead to uncertainty and failure to achieving benefits—and can potentially engender more problems.

Even if reuse is not your primary concern, you need to understand dependencies and interrelationships to determine the impact of change. Reliable and maintainable systems can only be built if there is a way to understand these impacts. The ability to catalog and categorize your enterprise's growing portfolio of services through inception, implementation, deployment, and operation make services easier to leverage and manage. By registering services, associated artifacts, and their relationships and dependencies, you can manage the impact of change when it is necessary to version a service. A SOA System of Record (SoR) is a key enabler for this.

You can only effectively achieve the planning, collaboration, management, and governance functions necessary to support successful SOA adoption by having complete visibility into the service portfolio. The infrastructure required to support these functions are SOA Service Registries and Repositories. This chapter explores how SOA Registries and Repositories act as the necessary building blocks for a successful SOA initiative.

KEY RECOMMENDATIONS:

- Recognize the importance of documenting and maintaining a formal System of Record (SoR) of your services, their revisions, and their service level agreements (SLA's).

- Understand the difference between a Service Registry and a Service Repository.

- Put a SoR in place for control and visibility before you need it.

- Reconcile your use of a SOA SoR with your existing Software Development Lifecycle Control (SDLC) system.

- Go further than just acquiring a Registry and Repository system. Plan how you are going to use and maintain it.

3.1 The SOA System Of Record

SOA Service Registries and Repositories combined provide your organization with a SOA SoR. A SOA SoR helps to manage, promote usage, and prevent duplication. It is the essential discovery capability that organizes services and related artifacts for use throughout the design or runtime phases of a service's lifecycle.

It is critical to effectively coordinate service developers, consumers, and stakeholders—including line of business analysts; those responsible for manufacturing and delivery activities such as application architects, testers and developers; and those responsible for operations. Most important, providing stakeholders with an integrated set of tools, each focused on their specific needs, helps organizations collaborate more effectively.

The goal of a SOA service-centric SoR is to help the enterprise (i.e., enterprise architects, service providers, and consumers) gain visibility into the SOA service portfolio. A SOA SoR enables an organization to determine what business services are available; identify which services the organization can use; and assess the impact business requirement changes have on existing processes. In other words, a SOA SoR helps organizations achieve agility.

A SOA SoR has two complementary components: A SOA Service Registry and a SOA Repository.

The SOA Service Registry

The SOA Service Registry is an index of deployed services. It holds references to service information, including the description of the service's interface, behavioral policies, and the means to inform a consuming application (which in turn may be a service) of an update to registry information, etc. It also specifies the location of the point of access for a service within a deployment environment. Specifically, the SOA Service Registry contains the following data:

- Descriptive metadata that might describe the operational status of the service.
- Deployment configuration information such as whether there is a service proxy.
- Authoritative descriptions of the service's configuration that enable applications, administrators, or deployment staff to understand deployment characteristics.

The SOA ecosystem components use the Service Registry to understand and interact with services. A service registry should be co-located with each environment you deploy, such as internal (company only) environments and/or shared environments that expose available services to third parties. In order to be registered in an SOA Service Registry, the service must be deployed, whether it is in a development environment, a component integration or system integration environment, or a pre-production or production environment.

Some vendors claim that their SOA Registry/Repository play a dual role of carrying out registry functions and storing data (i.e., the repository function) that relates to the description and design of the service rather than strictly describing a deployment. Combining design and deployment within a single registry/repository makes it difficult to manage service information across multiple deployment environments. More importantly, that approach leads to a situation where a developer can inadvertently make a change to a production environment. It is necessary to separate design from deployment to prevent the development team from making a change to a production system. Look to a SOA Repository to support your design needs.

The SOA Repository

Supporting the many tools that manage the lifecycle of a service, the SOA Repository provides a definitive and complete view of the service for stakeholders, including service providers, and consumers. It represents a SoR for the design and definition of your SOA. Using the SOA Repository, you can control and manage data and metadata associated with the service, including changes to either. It also offers services for transitioning between lifecycle stages.

The SOA Repository is the place where you find information about a service and pointers to where you can find additional information. Within the SOA Repository, you can expect to find the actual service interface description (the WSDL document and XML Schema documents) as well as documentation describing important information including:

- Functional and design specifications of a service
- Terms of use
- Sample messages
- Test plans and results
- Performance reports

Also, look for information relating to the organization responsible for the operations of the service, points of contact, and key stakeholders. You will also find metadata such as the service lifecycle state, functional and architectural metadata, the location of instances in various environments (by virtue of being integrated with SOA Service Registries), and the policies (and the content of the policies) that constrain or describe the behavior of a service.

A SOA Repository helps you organize and understand service relationships, dependencies, deployments, and descriptions across design and runtime environments. It includes application specific configurations, shared services, and the SOA service infrastructure. This helps you govern the set of business policies and processes that enable consistency and quality of operation for the systems that compose the SOA framework and its services. Using a SOA Repository puts you in a better position to manage the lifecycle of SOA services and the associated SOA. It reduces costs associated with duplication and errors in building these services. It also simplifies the process of deploying and maintaining systems.

In summary, the SOA Service Registry helps you understand the deployment and description of your service within a given environment. When extended by a repository, the registry turns your SOA into a well documented and governed ecosystem of services and consumers.

3.2 Buy Versus Build

Many who have embarked on a service-orientation project have wondered whether they should buy or build an SOA System of Record. To be successful with a SOA, an organization must achieve agility through the use of reusable service assets. Success depends on your ability to coordinate business services that are implemented and deployed. This is not a task for the faint of heart.

Some organizations start to create their SOA SoR using a spreadsheet. But this quickly becomes unmanageable. Others extend their LDAP identity management system, only to have their dream of directory enabled computing disappear when identity management take priority over application concerns. Some gravitate to platform discovery specifications such as DISCO and WSIL. Others embrace SDA Libraries, CMDBs or registry/repository standards. And some build their own registry, repository, or combination of the two.

Whatever you consider, you must focus on providing an infrastructure that is inclusive of both your stakeholders and their tools—that implies complying with standards. Remember, you are not in the business of developing tools, but rather enabling business capability.

SOA Service Registries

The following standards will enable you to avoid lock-in and gain flexibility. To describe your deployed services using a Service Registry, you need a standard method for the following activities.

- Enabling, publishing, and discovering service consumers, providers, and connection contracts.
- Classifying, relating, and storing business, technical, and policy information.
- Communicating and accessing services across heterogeneous, loosely-coupled systems.

The undisputed standard for a SOA Service Registry is Universal Description, Discovery, and Integration (UDDI). UDDI defines a set of services that support the description and discovery of the following:

- Businesses, organizations, and other Web services providers
- Web services
- Technical interfaces used to access those services

Based on a common set of industry standards, including HTTP, XML, XML Schema, and SOAP, UDDI provides an interoperable, foundational infrastructure based on a Web services software environment for both internal and public services.

SOA Repositories

Your SOA Repository is the catalyst that brings your stakeholders together and promotes collaboration. First, ensure that the SOA Repository you choose is entirely integrated with your UDDI service registries to provide a view of operational, deployment, and integration capabilities. In addition to carrying out the functions described in the previous section, your SOA Repository should also support the following:

- Organization and an understanding of your SOA service relationships, dependencies, deployments, and descriptions across the service's lifecycle. It should also manage the service's lifecycle and integrate the activities of your stakeholders with the goal to help you adapt to inevitable change.

- Employment of governance functions that help you manage policies that drive interoperability and reuse, as well as promote agility – though this is not entirely necessary to get started.

- Development of advanced reports to help you understand the state of affairs such as levels of compliance by producers and usage by consumers.

- Service level management functions that help coordinate consumer and provider service level expectations and ensure that service levels are met through integration with your management platform.

- Control and management of change of service definitions to ensure the best quality of data and information to all that depend on it.

Best of Breed Versus Vendor Specific

There are a number of robust, best-of-breed registry and repository products on the market today. As this functionality becomes better understood in the overall software community, parts of it are being incorporated into a wider set of products as a complementary capability. An example would be a software development system that is provided by an ERP application provider for developing extensions to their base application. As a result, many organizations are coming to terms with the inevitability of having more than one registry and repository. Thus the need to support standards becomes increasingly important.

In considering the use of these products, the following issues should be taken into account:

- Using multiple SoR systems increases the difficulty of finding information on a specific service since the location of the information may not be clear.

- Differing SoR systems may have different features, making life more difficult for the developer who needs access to both.

- Many SoR systems that come with larger packaged applications are designed to be used only for the services associated with that specific product. For example, they sometimes require the use of specific software development tools for that environment.

- The federation of SoR systems with automatic sharing or synchronization of information cannot be taken for granted, even if they both support the same version of the standards.

In general, a vendor who specializes on a topic, including this one, will push the state of the art forward more aggressively than one who pursues a broader agenda. On the other hand, a vendor who incorporates a SoR system into their larger development environment will build more automation between the different components of their specific environment.

3.3 Getting Started

Your SOA visibility and control initiative can be successful if the fundamentals receive the right attention. Remember, the goal is to bring together as many stakeholders as possible—including service developers and consumers, those with upcoming projects, and those that build, evolve, maintain, and operate the services and the supporting infrastructure. With this perspective, keep in mind that you are developing a methodology that will serve multiple projects, and that will maintain an accurate SoR of the combined work over time. You will find that a disciplined methodology is well worth the extra effort.

The following is an example set of steps that will start you on the right path:

Step 1: Establish a shared vision.
- Identify the scope, value, and business cases behind your initial implementation.
- Bring stakeholders together so they can understand the proposed services, their interrelationships, and the goal of the entire system.

Step 2: Design your services.
Define a set of services that meet the needs of your business. Consider the following steps:

- Identify appropriate services: Focus on coarse-grained and business oriented services as your early target.
- Capture the target design and its artifacts in your SOA SoR. Define the relationships between the services to support your initiative and create your taxonomies to organize this information.
- Provide team members with comprehensive interactive access to all artifacts.

- Leverage your SOA SoR as early as possible to get all stakeholders in agreement.

Step 3: Take inventory.
- Once you achieve a shared vision and identify the required services, review your 'as is' service portfolio and identify any reuse opportunities from previous work.
- Analyze and classify the existing services and related artifacts. Determine if they can be used 'as is' or whether modification is required.

Step 4: Plan stages that lead to your target implementation.
You won't get there all at once. Consider the following stages:
- Identify early opportunities to deliver value with coarse-grained and business-oriented services.
- Identify and prioritize risks (both technological and organizational) in transforming the existing system to your target implementation.
- Balance the delivery of value with reduction of risk in the early stages.
- Specify objective completion criteria for each stage of your project—identify risks, mitigate risks, and focus on delivering value.
- Establish policies and workflows that will govern the implementation of each stage.
- Provide team members with comprehensive, interactive access to all milestones, status, and artifacts.

Step 5: Manage the implementation of each stage.
- Implement planned services and applications, complying with policies, workflows, and contracts.
- Measure usage and seek feedback from stakeholders.
- Control change.
- Exploit knowledge gained by frequently updating your target architecture, service definitions, service interactions, expected results, and risk factors.
- Continue to provide team members with comprehensive, interactive access to all implementation information and artifacts.

Step 6: Ensure and promote service utilization.
Identify techniques and incentives that ensure and promote service utilization. Consider the following actions:
- Predict, measure, and compensate providers and consumers for operational costs such as hosting and maintenance.
- Foster confidence among providers and consumers by establishing a contract, discoverable policies, workflows, and visibility metrics.
- Establish team incentives by establishing metrics-driven recognition and awards.

At every step, focus on leveraging your SOA SoR to support the needs of your stakeholders and your initiatives.

3.4 SOA And The Software Development Lifecycle

SOA is a new form of software development, but many of the traditional issues relating to the software development process still apply. However, services have somewhat different characteristics than 'application oriented' development. Registries and repositories can provide significant benefits in supporting a software development lifecycle (SDLC) framework for services. This section explains how.

Those who successfully implement an SOA realize that key ingredients include visibility, collaboration, trust, and control of the business services that they build, operate, and maintain. For example:

- **Visibility.** If prospective service consumers can't easily discover business service assets and identify their attributes, such as their operational characteristics, the promise of SOA is largely lost.

- **Collaboration.** Service orientation drives significantly increased need for collaboration between service providers and consumers, operations teams, as well as the business analysts, architects, and development teams that define and evolve the services. Organizations can adopt SOA techniques and products to build and deploy a service infrastructure, but their efforts will flounder without controls for ensuring consistency and interoperability.

- **Trust**. If there is a lack of trust between organizations there will be hesitancy to use a service that others control. A key goal in your SOA journey is to find ways to promote trust between stakeholders and increase confidence by providing control and visibility of the service. You need to enable providers to analyze the effect of change and maintain a balance between the costs and benefits of a change and its impact on consumers.

- **Control**. You will also need to equip yourself and your enterprise architects with control capabilities. You'll want to enforce guidelines that facilitate interoperability and consistency without creating manually intensive processes that slow SOA adoption. You'll also want to implement management capabilities that drive compliance with policies for service implementation, operational policies, and best practices.

As you move towards service orientation, keep in mind that your goal is to drive collaboration. Development and test teams that have adopted software development lifecycle methodologies need to ensure that everyone understands the service in the same way to facilitate increased reuse, better failure recovery, and easier evolution of the service.

3.4.1 Example Service Development Lifecycle

The following is an example of creating a service that will provide your organization with visibility and control. For the sake of brevity, we do not include the consumer's view of the lifecycle activities relating to discovering a service; due-diligence activities relating to the decision to use the service; and the requisite service-level activities. Note that few organizations in the real world fully adopt all of these activities in the disciplined way as listed below.

Step 1: Identify need for a new business service.
A business analyst identifies the need for a new business service. The analyst then creates a placeholder in his SOA System of Record to inform prospective consumers that a new business service is in early stages of definition and implementation.

Step 2: Create a new project.
A project manager generates a request for the creation of a new project using a project and portfolio management tool to create the project definition, allocate resources, and manage the project.

Step 3: Employ a software development asset libarary.
Once the service production project is approved, funded, and staffed, the development team uses tools such as a software development asset (SDA) library or team Wiki. The development team uses these tools to manage the software development lifecycle (SDLC) of the service, better collaborate, and to implement for example checkpoints in the process to control the SDLC.

Step 4: Begin service development.
Service development begins. The developer uses an IDE of choice to implement the service, and the SOA Repository to search for services he needs to consume and their associated artifacts. The developer uses the SOA Repository to register consumption of these services in order to alert the service provider of new dependencies.

Step 5: Track and report development efforts.
The activities executed by the development team are reported into the project and portfolio tool. At appropriate points during manufacturing, the SOA Repository is updated with lifecycle information relating to the state of the service under development.

Step 6: Store artifacts in a SCMS.
Service implementation artifacts are stored in the organization's source control management system (SCMS). A source code management system manages physical artifacts such as WSDLs, Java files, and DLLs.

Step 7: Track and manage implantation and testing.
During the implementation and testing of the service, SDLC tools of choice are used (e.g., requirements management, quality management, and defect tracking).

Step 8: Submit service approval and deployment.
As part of the SDLC process, the development team submits the service for approval; conformance to design-time policies is reviewed; test and quality metrics are reviewed; and upon successful test and certification, a

community of consumers approves the service for deployment and use. The service and information regarding the set of associated proxies (e.g., service management and security appliances) are then registered in the SOA Service Registry.

Step 9: Deploy service for consumption.
Consumption and service-level management activities begin. These support the enablement and provisioning of consumption, the establishment and enablement of service levels, and capacity planning.

As a result of this process, artifacts and relationships were created between the service, its stakeholders, and their tools. Now you need to consider how you will support prospective consumers in their decision to use a service. You also need to know where to turn when a problem occurs to gain an understanding of the relationships between the service definition, its components, and deployment information. The toolset you turn to is a SOA SoR.

3.5 Conclusion

Service orientation is a journey. Success requires transformation. In particular, you must provide visibility into the environment you're developing, encourage trust between developers and consumers of services, and empower your organization to control the evolution of a service-oriented infrastructure and architecture.

Don't try to boil the ocean. Start small and focus on developing methodologies along with visibility and control operations that will help stakeholders collaborate better. Be inclusive—seek out your stakeholders. Get them to participate in building and helping you sustain a SOA SoR and impress upon them that everyone has a stake in it.

CHAPTER 4

Enterprise Service Buses

Hub Vandervoort
Chief Technology Officer
Progress Software

The chain of logic supporting the value of a service-oriented architecture (SOA) begins with the principal objective to accelerate time-to-value of IT assets (see Figure 4.1). A SOA accomplishes this by better aligning the functions (or services) performed by IT with their driving business objectives. A SOA enables stronger alignment through greater agility. It enables flexibility of IT supported business processes and rapid reuse of IT resources across a broader number of business functions. Further down this chain of logic, a SOA should support agile reuse by facilitating easier, faster and broader integration derived from IT standards that promote higher levels of native interoperability between services.

This logic presumes that by employing interoperability standards everything would be intrinsically integrated and not require additional integration to make them work together. However, this assumption predicates that the standards are fully comprehensive to address all dimensions of interoperability and that uniform standards are employed across all the inter-working elements—both of which are often questionable assumptions in any large scale SOA environment.

Figure 4.1: SOA Value Chain

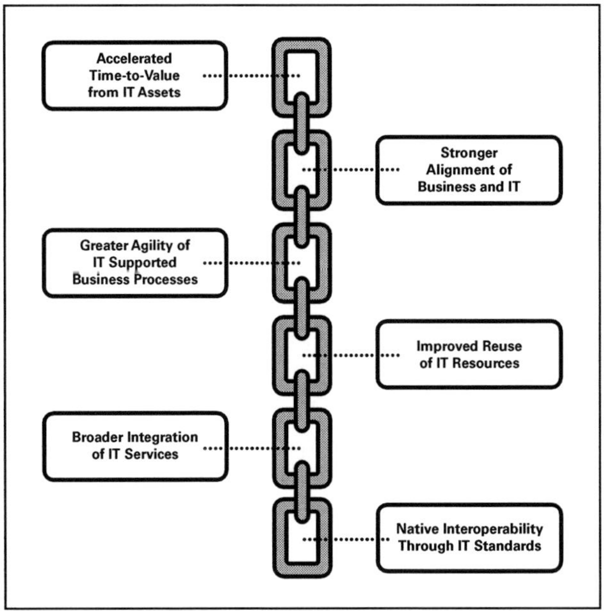

KEY RECOMMENDATIONS:

- Develop a solid understanding of the capabilities and limitations of the basic web services request/reply protocols versus the enhanced capabilities of an ESB.

- Analyze your interoperability issues and determine whether you will need an ESB to reconcile incompatibilities.

- Understand the different kinds of ESB's and which would be best for you.

- Think through what "role" you want an ESB to play in your system.

- Decide what forms of "mediation" you want from your ESB.

This is where an Enterprise Service Bus (ESB) comes in. An ESB is an infrastructure platform that fills critical interoperability gaps left open in state-of-the-art standards. More importantly, it enables interoperability across dissimilar standards which often exist in modern computing environments. Along the way, it brings a higher level of robustness to the infrastructure necessary to meet the mission-critical performance, reliability and scalability needed by contemporary enterprises.

4.1 Introduction To ESBs

A Closer Look At Interoperability

In the SOA logic chain, interoperability is the predicate to agility and reuse. However, 'true' interoperability must be assessed on multiple dimensions, all of which must be in alignment between services if genuine interoperability is to occur. These dimensions of alignment fall into four broad categories: Functional, Structural, Behavioral and Performance.

For a consumer service to use a particular provider service, it must be aligned on the functional requirements. The provider must do what the consumer wants, whether it's computing a price, looking up a customer, updating and order or responding to an event of interest. While the functionality is up to the service, there are other considerations which may or may not be handled by the service itself.

- **Structural**. Structural or systemic, alignment might be thought of as aligning the 'pin-outs' of an interface. If the pins between a printer and the PC don't match, the printer won't print, even if your PC is perfectly capable of driving a serial printer. In SOA, this type of alignment is manifest in the protocols and formats employed by the consumer and provider services. They must align precisely or interoperability will not occur, even if the provider delivers the correct function.

- **Behavioral.** Behavioral alignment extends to more intangible notions such as semantics and interaction. With respect to semantics, a consumer service may request a 'customer' business object, but the provider service produces business objects called 'party' and types the object with an attribute enumerated as customer, vendor, partner, supplier, etc. While the provider is capable of producing the desired information, and the 'pins are in alignment', the interpretation of the produced result may or may not be natively intelligible by the consumer because the semantics are different. Similarly, with respect to interaction, there may be a consumer that wants to 'inquire' for customers when needed, while there may be a provider service that wants to 'publish' customer business objects each time one is created or updated. Although all other aspects of interoperability may be in alignment, if one wants to ask for customers and another wants to broadcast them on particular events, there still won't be interoperability because the behavior of dialog is out of alignment.

- **Performance.** Performance encompasses issues beyond direct interoperability; these are considerations having to do with Quality-of-Service (QoS) and Quality-of-Protection (QoP), or simply the entire realm of service-level and security-policy. Alignment here is equally critical. If a provider service was built to handle 2 requests per second with 1 second response time, consumers must be aligned with that service-level expectation or realistic production interoperability cannot be achieved. Likewise, if a provider service was deployed with the expectation that it would only be consumed by internal services, and was then inadvertently exposed for consumption by a public audience, it would be out of alignment with expected security policy.

The point to all of this is that real-world interoperability is only possible when all aspects of alignment are achieved. However, the choice of where to implement the last three of these categorical considerations is critical to the question of reuse. While the functional aspects of interoperability indeed rest entirely with the services themselves, if the services also take on the responsibility for structural, behavioral and performance related concerns, reuse erodes rapidly and the chain of logic supporting SOA unravels.

If services were left to 'fend for themselves' on all these points they would either come up short on support for requirements essential to certain contexts or they would become increasingly bulky . Moreover, the services would be more costly to develop, operate and maintain and would lead to duplication of those capabilities across multiple services with inconsistencies between them.

On the other hand, services that indeed delegate all these considerations entirely to common infrastructure, become inherently more reusable across more contexts and thus become more agile and manageable at scale—preserving the SOA chain of logic. ESB is this common infrastructure onto which a service can delegate mediation of these concerns. Simply put, ESB is a mediation layer for enterprise SOA whose express purpose is to mediate differences in structural, behavioral and performance characteristics between services.

ESB extends the basic idea of abstraction between participants (providers and consumers) to enterprise scale. ESB permits services (consumers and providers) to interact in a loosely-coupled manner; more so than if they were simply connected point-to-point using the most contemporary loose-coupled standard protocols, like WebServices or Java Message Service, alone. This enables services, and the processes that use them, to change over time, at a faster rate and to a much greater degree, without affecting other services or processes around them.

This is the foundation for agility.

The Paradigm Shift

The ESB architecture approaches the problem based on several core principles:

- **Declarative, Meta-data, Policy or Configuration –Driven.**
  As opposed to integration within the services themselves, an ESB does not usually require one to 'program' integration. Rather, interoperability is configured, most of the time through standards, permitting integrations to be changed in-place, without having to return to the developer to 'version' the application (and repeat the design, code, test and deploy life-cycle for the change). The net effect is that change is more agile.

- **Light-weight Deployment and Execution Models**
  This principle, if adhered to correctly, actually manifests in the technology as discrete separable elements that consume less resource in aggregate. Functions are not repeated within each service and required functions are installed when and where needed.

- **Distributed/Federated Life-cycle Support.**
  A robust ESB will always manage as one logical entity despite being deployed across many machines in diverse locations. One can debug processes, perform configuration updates and deploy new services and functionality, as well as apply policies and take measurements across the entire network of participating elements, with nearly all of the convenience and control one expects from a monolithic stack on a single machine—only in this case, potentially spread across the globe.

Taken together, these characteristics position ESB as a key foundational element of a large-scale SOA—it becomes a mechanism for not only technical loose-coupling but also enables notions of 'organizational loose coupling'— permitting agility without a loss of governance or control. An ESB can support federation—where independent domains can interoperate without sacrificing their independence while also achieving interoperation and visibility.

4.2 When To Use An ESB

In terms of SOA adoption, one might ask, when does ESB become important? This can be summarized in three simple rules of thumb:

Rule 1: When the number of interdependencies between Services, Processes and Schemas, becomes more than twice the aggregate number of those elements.

Practically speaking, this is when the inventory of processes, services and schemas approaches 50. Mediating interrelationships between SOA elements is the critical focus—arguably the most critical success factor: Managing 'N-square complexity'.

SOA operates at a much finer granularity than integration of traditional monolithic applications. Simply put, there will be more services than there were applications. As a result, interdependencies accumulate much faster then before. If these are not managed early, they get out of control very quickly and raise the cost of operating and maintaining the SOA, eventually eclipsing the cost of the approach you were trying to replace.

Services are related by the transport they use, the processes they participate in, the semantics and interaction model they share and so on. If each of these is established in a point-to-point manner, the number of mediations grows exponentially to the number of services, process and schemas. Alternatively, if each of the processes, schemas and services has only one set of relationships to consider—the ones it has to the ESB—the number of mediations always remains proportionate and grows linearly in relation to the number of services (see Figure 4.2).

Figure 4.2: Service Reuse Linearity

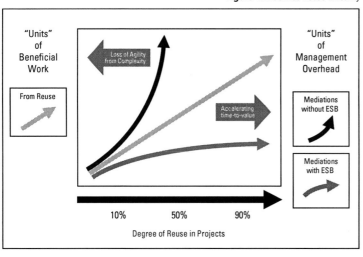

The benefits of SOA begin to appear through reuse of common services and schemas across processes. Using an ESB to mediate the structural, behavioral, and performance interoperability dimensions will result in 'units' of beneficial work growing at a faster rate than 'units' of management overhead associated with new mediations. Time to value will accelerate.

Rule 2: When the process objectives of the SOA begin to span multiple geographically distributed locations and/or federated organizational boundaries.

This generally becomes essential between 5 and 10 locations, although federation drivers will become acute sooner than distribution (i.e., as few as three federated parties). This stems from the fact that technologically, both are hard to manage and neither problem is satisfied entirely by a single product.

Distribution conjures up system considerations that are not evident when integration scope is confined to a LAN in one location. Encryption, tunneling, firewall and proxy traversal, as well as questions of latency, availability and routing introduce substantial infrastructure into the equation. Without an ESB in place to hide this, the complexity of managing quality of service across all the additional components ripples back into the services and processes themselves.

Federation exacerbates complexity. It is reasonable to expect federation to follow distribution—the more distributed an enterprise becomes the more likely it is to be federated organizationally. The situation now involves crossing security domains, as well as realms of autonomous process, service and data ownership, at least to some degree. This introduces still more heterogeneous infrastructure to allow cross-domain users to share and manage assets as a group, without compromising sovereignty over their own domain.

To appreciate this completely, compare the alternatives. Clearly, the simplest technical solution would be to collapse all the participating member domains into a single operational/security domain and obviate the federation issue altogether. Unfortunately, this is rarely possible in political terms. Alternatively, one could employ classic B2B techniques and allow domains to interoperate through exchange patterns. While B2B does support interoperability through exchange messages, it does not offer any support for cross-domain change management and deployment coordination, nor does it provide control or measurement over spanning processes—aspects that are essential to effective enterprise function like global financial roll-up, integrated purchasing, sharing of common data, uniform application of policy, and so on.

Certain ESBs meet these two perspectives in the middle by permitting the notion of 'multi-segmented operations', which enables independent governance domains to coexist in relationships that are more transparent that B2B provides, without obviating the autonomy of independent operating areas.

Rule 3: When you need to integrate services using disparate interaction models.

This essentially points out that services will be constructed to 'speak' in a particular interaction style that must be reconciled if dissimilar ones are going to communicate freely. Jon Udell, InfoWorld chief analyst, has an expression: "Request-driven software speaks when spoken to; event-driven software speaks when it has something to say". The difference would keep the two (request-driven and event-driven software) from interacting if something didn't provide a translation in the middle.

In ESB terms, mediating interaction model means that whether a service speaks through request-reply, publish-subscribe, store-and-forward, or batch files, they can be enabled to interact, despite the 'impedance mismatch'. This is an incredibly powerful concept as it relates to technical reuse.

4.3 Selecting An ESB Product

There are two prevailing implementation architectures, or embodiments, for ESB. Most conform to either a proxy/gateway or broker-oriented model, which more-or-less reflects the choice for where ESB execution components reside.

Proxy/Gateway-oriented Or Broker-oriented ESB Architectures

Roughly half the ESB products choose a standard container environment as a host (i.e., J2EE, Servlet, .NET, etc.). ESB components conform to the container paradigm and either co-resides with services in the same container or is positioned in a separate instance of a like container. Services interact with the ESB in a consistent component architecture and the general deployment pattern resembles a proxy or gateway.

The other half of the market chooses a stand-alone execution environment for the ESB. While these certainly make accommodations for standard containers (to varying degree and depth), they do not depend on them, and thus, tend to exhibit greater neutrality among containers types rather than having implicit affinity to only one type of container. The pattern of deployment in this case most resembles a broker. Services interact with the ESB directly through open service interfaces.

Stemming from the choice of host environment, ESB products exhibit certain styles that associate with this implementation difference.

Application-centric Versus Integration-centric Styles

The first of these is application-centric vs. integration-centric. In any ESB, two sub-systems stand prominent: the Service Container and the Messaging/Communication sub-system. Vendors tend to weight the importance of these differently—some placing greater emphasis on messaging, others on the service container. While none take the bias to an extreme, the market is decidedly split.

The application-centric group bases its ESB architectures around a specific standard container. The attractive quality in this orientation is its high degree of alignment between the ESB and a particular service or application design methodology and tooling, and is thus most often selected by application teams.

The integration-oriented group is clustered among those using a broker-oriented model that disassociates from any particular container architecture. The design center bias toward the messaging aspects of the platform is mostly favored by integration teams with responsibility for SOA across heterogeneous application and service platforms. While offering generally less intimate integration with any one application design platform, its neutrality, as well as generally superior support for distribution, federation and events, makes it attractive for solving 'cross-anything' challenges.

Service Orchestration Paradigm

The other distinguishing ESB style has to do with the 'control-of-flow' semantics employed for sequencing, decision making and error-recovery logic—its service orchestration paradigm.

Some ESBs favor a central coordinator that sequences service invocations as request/reply interactions. This command-and-control oriented behavior provides for straight forward composition that resembles traditional top-down, block-oriented programming.

The contrasting approach formulates process sequence through event-passing. This alternative organizes services to 'listen' to particular event channels across which events are emitted as publish/subscribe, one-way or store-and-forward interactions. This approach to process composition shifts more of the decision logic out to the services but offers a broader range of modeling options. Event-based processes can be visually rendered as block-oriented, event-exchange, or complex correlation patterns—more sophisticated models for process that are valuable in cross-organization integration and high-speed event-driven architecture (EDA) style applications (e.g. Program Trading, Power/Plant Management, RFID, BAM, etc.)

Since neither approach is comprehensive, both prove to be useful and are thus supported to one extent or another by all types of ESB. However, vendor implementations decidedly favor one approach over the other.

ESB Form Factors

A range of ESB packaging options have evolved, each with unique strengths and weaknesses (see Figure 4.3)

4.4 Applications Of An ESB

While an ESB can be applied in countless ways, the simplest organization for thinking about this is around the roles it can play. This follows one of four specific patterns, none of which are mutually exclusive. Each pattern notionally establishes a type of 'channel'. These channels serve a particular purpose or role in the enterprise SOA. Channels are characterized by the nature of the messages they carry and the interaction models they employ. The four patterns, or channel types, are:

- Interaction Channel
- Process Channel
- Information Channel
- Event Channel

ESB TYPE	DESCRIPTION	STRENGTH	WEAKNESS
AD HOC (roll-your-own)	An assemblage of licensed or home-grown subsystems comprising an ESB, namely support for: MOM, Web Services, Transformation and Intelligent Routing capabilities, along side some container architecture	• Potential Initial Savings • Fit to Requirement • Potential Performance Advantage in unique applications	• Must architect/build: security, management, development tools and deployment support. • Potentially higher overall TCO
PACKAGED/ COMMERCIAL (licensed software)	Complete (or semi-complete) Out-of-Box platforms that usually include the principal components of an ESB but may not provide complete Management Life-cycle and security capability. Some commercial ESBs also separate out support for MOM, depending on other vendor or third-party products for this capability.	• Generally more mature / proven offerings • Unique vendor advantages • More complete enterprise support • Larger developer/ISV ecosystem	• Potentially Higher initial cost (but likely lower lifetime TCO) • Concerns over vendor lock-in and/or future direction/viability • Vendor alignment with specific industry or use-case requirements
OPEN SOURCE (licensed software)	Similar to Commercial ESBs but developed in an Open Source or Community-Edition model. The latter however is often a free 'introductory-version' to a commercially licensed upgrade, that is intended to seed community development for the commercial offering and thus should not be confused with true open source licensing models.	• Open Source community and ecosystem advantages • Lower initial cost (potentially lower TCO) • Greatest Standards Conformity/Openness • Potentially lower risk of technology 'lock-in'	• Generally less mature/ proven • Questionable enterprise support policies and/or technical capabilities (i.e. performance, scalability, reliability)
HARDWARE/ APPLIANCE	Specialized hardware device that is hardened and optimized for discrete lower-level ESB operations, especially transport mediation and XML parsing (i.e. XML transformation, simple content-based routing, WSDL validations, SLA management, Security, etc.)	• Potentially higher performance and scalability on specialized functions • Generally simpler management (i.e., operations & network-engineer friendly)	• Potentially higher cost • Lacks advanced ESB capabilities (e.g. semantics, service orchestration, etc.) • Disjointed management (e.g. separate from the process or application environment)
ESB AS A SERVICE Utility/ Software-as-a-Service (SaaS)	ESB functionality offered by a third-party, network-based provider. Most often offered in a SaaS, Managed Hosting or Outsource model by a Systems Integrator, ISP or Telecommunications Carrier. Examples include: • EDS, AirSOA, an ESB for the Airline Industry sold as an outsourced, managed-service • British Telecom, BT iBus, an ESB marketed as a telecom service (dial-tone), which is provisioned through specialized customer-premises hardware and billed as a subscription (monthly) service.	• Low/Zero initial capital expense; potentially lower TCO • Faster initial implementation • Minimal internal requirements (e.g. training, hardware, related systems, etc.) • Potentially better support for B2B and industry-specific applications/use-cases	• Less Mature as a business model (although generally based on similar technology) • Potentially narrower range of support capabilities (i.e., little customization of packaged services) • Potential security risks

PATTERN: Interaction Channel	USAGE SCENARIO: Remote Information Access
INDUSTRY	**USE-CASES**
Insurance	Agency store-front portals, self-service enrollment/claims inquiry
Financial Services	Remote Trader Workstations, Portfolio management portals
Telecommunications	Customer Provisioning/Self-Service, Call Centers
Manufacturing	Supplier Portals, ERP Portals, Product Catalogs
Retail	Multi-Channel Marketing, Supplier (VMI) Portals
Transportation	Package Tracking, Reservations Portals
Government	Citizens Services Portal, Cross-Agency Portals (e.g. Justice, HS, DMV)

PATTERN: Process Channel	USAGE SCENARIO: Continuous Pipeline Processing
Insurance	Claims processing, underwriting
Financial Services	Front-/Mid-office Straight through processing—STP (T+1, T+0)
Telecommunications	Operational Support Services (OSS),
Manufacturing	ERP, Supply-Chain/Procurement Management
Retail	Supply Chain Replenishment, Custom pack/assembly operations
Transportation	Inventory and Supply Chain/Procurement Management,
Government	Enrollment, Licensing, Justice, Human Services, Defense Logistics

PATTERN: Information Channel	USAGE SCENARIO: Remote Information Distribution
INDUSTRY	**USE-CASES**
Insurance	Policy Master distribution (e.g. claims centers and branch offices)
Financial Services	Securities Master distribution (e.g. to trading desks)
Telecommunications	Circuit Inventory and Customer Master data distribution
Manufacturing	Product & Inventory Master Distribution
Retail	Price Master and Customer Master Distribution
Transportation	Flight Operations and Inventory Status distribution
Government	Citizen Master, Tax/Property records, OFAC/Patriot Act data distribution

PATTERN: Event Channel	USAGE SCENARIO: Real-time Response to Business Events
Insurance	Claims alerting, New customer alerts, emergency monitoring
Financial Services	Real-time Market Data, Fraud Surveillance, Compliance monitoring
Telecommunications	NMS Alert, MPLS call detail and Point-of-presence notifications
Manufacturing	RFID/Auto-ID Track & Trace, Shop Floor control and monitoring (BAM)
Retail	RFID/Auto-ID Track & Trace, supply chain monitoring (BAM)
Transportation	Baggage/Cargo tracking, Airport/Flight-line operations, Emergency
Government	Emergency Services, Public Transit/Railway Monitoring, Admissions

Figure 4.4 summarizes Industry specific ESB use-case examples that are representative of each of these four channel types.

Interaction Channel

As an interaction channel, ESB is positioned to participate in the flow of interaction by mediating exchanges between 'front-end' consumer services, through to back-end process- and data-oriented provider services. Gartner refers to this as Interactive or Uniform SOA and associates it with services operating in portals or controlling rich-client, mobility and alternate user interfaces channel (ATMs, Kiosks, IVRs, etc.)

From a usage scenario point of view, this pattern can be thought of as 'Remote Information Access' where a composite application begins to need real-time access to multiple back-end systems. ESB indicators strengthen when back-ends are heterogeneous, distributed and federated organizationally and/or there is the need for multi-channel user interface support (i.e., more than just browsers).

This pattern tends to favor the application centric and command-control oriented ESB styles for its close affinity with application servers on which portals and user interface logic are usually hosted. However, care should be taken to avoid solving short-term problems by aligning the ESB architecture too closely to the portal host —for quick initial delivery—only to discover that the environment evolves to become considerably more distributed and/or federated, which would favor a message oriented ESB.

Process Channel

In this role, the ESB behaves in an orchestration-centric manner, where its purpose is to mediate services along a business process pipeline. While BPM often sits above this type of SOA-level orchestration (to mediate human interaction and long-running processes) ESB service orchestration performs fine-grain service sequencing for machine-to-machine interactions. Gartner refers to this role as Integration or Composite SOA.

This usage scenario might be thought of as 'Continuous Pipeline Processing', where processes are enabled to flow 'hands-free'. This scenario is intended to improve automation of a process pipeline, reduce latency between steps, improving information accuracy and integrity across stages, and increase agility in handling variable process decision routes. This scenario can be adeptly handled by either Application- or Message-centric ESBs, the patterns will be better served by message centric architectures in highly distributed landscapes.

Information Channel

As an Information Channel, the ESB role can be described as information-centric, where function is geared toward provider-side services. In this case, mediation is on behalf of back-end provider services exposed for data access and transactional purposes. ESB provides access to data services, where they would most likely be invoked by user-facing and process-control oriented consumer services elsewhere on the bus. ESB functions provide aggregation of federated back-end data and coordination of process-oriented business logic across data services.

This usage scenario is best described as 'Remote Information Distribution', where the motivation is distribution of master reference data (MRD) across remote services requiring a near-real-time 'single-version-of-the-truth'. This does not replace data warehouses and MRD applications; rather it compliments them by enabling distribution of master data to remote locations. This pattern introduces scalability by extending data onto the ESB virtually regardless of location. The pattern frequently replaces FTP, batch transfer techniques commonly employed to distribute MRD in order to improve the timeliness of remote updates. While either style of ESB could in theory support this usage, the message-centric class of ESB generally fits better given its superior distribution as well as pub/sub, store-and-forward, and event-processing support.

Event Channel

The event channel role is, as the name suggests, event-centric and oriented around the notion of syndication. Gartner refers to this as Event-Driven Architecture (EDA) or Notification-based SOA. The ESB purpose is to support a distributed fabric of event channels, distributed using publish and subscribe model of communication. Producer services publish messages (events) of relative interest into this namespace and the bus mediates these events over to syndicated consumer services that subscribe to and act upon them. Typical usage scenarios are where organizations have many functions that need to 'Respond to Business Events in Real-time'—specifically when one type of event may be of interest to many different functional roles.

For example: When a plane lands at an airport, a number of interested parties must be alerted to take action—the tower must record it in a log; baggage handlers, fueling trucks and ground crews must all move into position; terminal displays must all be updated, and so on. If information had to be explicitly routed to each of the interested parties, there would be precipitous process maintenance required each time a new interested party joined the network. Using event-driven, publish/subscribe architectures, generators of events remain immune from changes in the set of syndicating parties. New consumers simply subscribe to channels of interest to receive real-time notification. Thus, the motivations for this pattern is when a large population of event-sources and event-sinks exist. As the name of this usage style suggests, this pattern clearly favors the event-centric ESB architecture.

Common Theme Applicable To All Channel Types

One interesting point to note is that, irrespective of the channel architecture, in roughly one-third of the ESB usage scenarios, the catalyst for ESB implementation is 'batch-to-real-time migration'. In the context of legacy systems modernization, a common model of integration, yester-year, was batch-oriented file transfer and extract-transform-load (ETL). While improvements to those technologies continue to come to market, the agility of loosely-coupled systems cannot be realized through set-oriented, batch processing—no matter how much you optimize the batch process. However, abrupt, flash-cut-over to event-oriented paradigms is usually not feasible for reasons of scale, scope, risk, cost and a myriad of other constraints. The journey from batch to real-time can only be accomplished in incremental steps. ESB therefore becomes the ideal assistant in that journey as its support for interaction model mediation permits a gradual shift to real-time SOA without the disruption or risk. As such, certain ESBs accentuate this application by either bundling or offering companion ETL capability to assist in the orchestration of file oriented process (like ETL), while at the same time providing means to parse data sets into individual transactions, or document-level granularity, for discrete handling on process flows.

4.5 Mediation And ESBs

It's All About Mediation

In the context of enterprise integration architecture, there are several mediations an ESB can provide. ESB mediates by acting as a third party intermediary that resolves differences between services in order to bring about agreement—which creates interoperability.

Comparable forms of mediation appear in the telephone network and public internet. The carrier network mediates the signaling protocols used by different phones and switches such that the differences are transparent to one another. Similarly, the Internet DNS service provides another form of mediation, 'location transparency', that allows abstract use of a domain name that is transparently mapped to a specific location (an IP address) on the Internet.

We can use these examples as metaphors to describe the types of mediation an ESB performs in an enterprise SOA. Specifically, the ESB provides seven types of mediation, labeled as follows: Transport, Destination, Semantic, Sequence (e.g. Service Orchestration), Error recovery, QoS/QoP, and Interaction model.

The importance of these mediations as a group has to do with a key link in the SOA logic chain—Reuse. In order to achieve optimal reuse, two things need to occur, technically:

- Services must be developed with the right level of functional granularity.
- Services must delegate mediation responsibility to infrastructure (i.e., not take on structural, behavioral and performance interoperability requirements itself).

When a service can depend on infrastructure to manage all the points of mediation, it has the greatest likelihood of reusability. ESB enables critical mediations to occur inside the infrastructure such that services can be written in a way that disregards any consideration of these mediations. Services maintain only one set of relationships—those it has with the bus—and the bus mediates these concerns to adapt to the specific variations that might be employed by another service.

First point of mediation: Transport

Generally any enterprise will have many different transports in use. While HTTP/SOAP-based WebServices may be an idealized end-state goal to normalize toward, two realities are true: First, for years to come, there will be many protocols in use that predated HTTP/SOAP; and second, by the time HTTP/SOAP would reach ubiquity, new protocols will have been invented that will optimize further on current state-of-the-art. Also, the WS-SOAP standards support countless variations in implementation leading to incompatible 'flavors'. While the WSI Basic Profile attempts to establish concrete interoperability around a least common denominator, the likelihood of widespread variations will undoubtedly exist in many cases. The enterprise SOA protocol set under consideration would likely include (HTTP/REST, WS-SOAP, RMI, JMS, CORBA, etc.)

In order to support integration at enterprise scale, one cannot predicate that a service supports interoperability among all the protocols in use on its own. Rather it should simply be able to 'on-ramp' to the enterprise using whatever transport it chooses to do so with, and rely on infrastructure to mediate it to other protocols. An ESB satisfies this objective by providing multiple levels of transport on- and off-ramps that support interoperability across all types of common protocols.

Second point of mediation: Destination

As noted earlier, the Internet provides location transparency and mediation. So why then does the ESB need to provide this capability again? In the case of the Internet, location transparency extends to only one single static address, usually associated with one physical machine or cluster—the domain address usually resolves to one single IP address. However, in enterprise SOA, the notion of location needs to become more robust, abstract and virtualized. At any given moment, a service may need to come up or down and be relocated on-the-fly, or exist in several places at once, yet it must exist logically under only one service name. Examples include load-balancing, distribution of instances of a given service to remote locations (e.g. stores, branches, trading desks, plants, warehouses, etc.) where they can execute closer to the business function being supported, and implementation of two services, one in a primary data center, another in a disaster recovery location. The most evolved example of this idea occurs in the case of so called 'follow the sun operations'. Here, services may become operational or taken off-line as workload shifts around the globe—as in trading operations of an investment bank. Here, a 'risk management' or 'compliance' service may be operational in London and New York when markets are open in those regions but as London closes for the day, the Tokyo service comes on line. Meanwhile, any process that uses the 'compliance service' simply references it by its logical name and the ESB infrastructure provides a routing to the most appropriate instance in the moment.

Third point of mediation: Semantics

Returning to the telephony metaphor, imagine if you will a situation where I spoke English but the person I wanted to call only spoke Chinese. In enterprise SOA, it would mean that every service would need to be fluent in all the languages spoken by every service it would be likely to interact with. This is a form of point-to-point integration that can kill a SOA agility and manageability quickly.

This is resolved by using the ESB infrastructure as a 'universal semantic translator'. Every service speaks to the ESB in whatever its own native (semantic) language might be and then the infrastructure maps that to a global/common (canonical) language, which only the infrastructure knows completely. Then, upon delivery to the other end, it maps the conversation once more to the appropriate dialect for the receiving party. Importantly, the common vocabulary is simply the intersection of the vocabularies of the interacting services, not the union of the service's entire grammar. The service can then be created without consideration for the language of its counterparty and thus can be reused in any context, irrespective of the language employed at the other end.

Fourth point of mediation: Sequencing

Too often, services are written with far too great an awareness of the processes they will be used in. In other words, services are frequently created with certain expectations of pre- and post-conditions that stipulate their order of execution relative to other services. It is not uncommon to see services even calling dependent services directly. Likewise, services frequently embody error-recovery logic that really belongs at the process level, not tucked inside the service itself.

As a design goal, it's not that services should always be prohibited from calling other services directly, whether for service orchestration or error recovery purposes. It is however a point of caution to make very judicious use of direct service invocations.

Once a service is 'hard-wired' to call another service, whether that call is conditional or not, it binds them together in such a way that they can no longer be used outside the context of both being employed together. While it might be determined that it is more efficient to have one service directly call the another than if it were to pass through a brokered intermediary like an ESB, it carries the consequence of limiting reuse of the first service because now it can only be employed when the second is also desired. At the end of the day, reuse value usually outweighs the value of any marginal performance gain achieved at the expense of reuse.

Sequencing is a form of Service Orchestration, or the ability to compose a sequence of multiple services into a composite service—whether for business process or error-recovery purposes. Thus, in order for services to be able to delegate these mediations to infrastructure, the infrastructure must provide mechanisms for composition and Service Orchestration. Most ESBs will provide a process composition framework. Most often, contemporary ESBs will offer support for WS-BPEL (WebServices—Business Process Execution Language), a standard grammar for process composition. However, it is important to also recognize that there is a distinct difference between BPM and Service-Orchestration, where architecturally speaking, they should not be used interchangeably.

BPEL would have been more aply named: SOL—Service-Orchestration Language. BPM is about people. BPEL is about Services

Fifth point of mediation: Error-Recovery

If each process failure in effect requires a 'recovery process' to deal with the anomaly, the problems of poor reuse will be exacerbated multiple times over if services also attempted to deal with error-recovery issues on it's own. Here is an example that illustrates how services attempting to take on error recovery themselves become contextually constrained to a point that reuse becomes severely compromised, making it difficult to fully visualize, manage and optimize.

A service tries to update a database with a service request that has been made against its interface. However, there is a network problem which prevents the service from connecting to the database. If the service were to incorporate its own error recovery logic, say to perform a retry some number of times, it hijacks the opportunity for the infrastructure to provide more advanced remediation; for example rerouting to another service that has a functional database connection. If the service were to take on the entire burden of understanding alternative strategies and being aware of all the possible retry locations in the network, it not only becomes contextually bound to that understanding of recovery but also becomes less location independent as well. Here, service orchestration, placed in the infrastructure and outside the service context, could be used to perform a wide range of recoveries.

Individual service errors can sometimes be handled by the service infrastructure (for example Try/Catch blocks of EJBs delegating transactional roll-back to their J2EE container or data service results provided by the information server cache when the source data is unavailable). An ESB operates at a scope that may encompass many heterogeneous services and containers across vast geographies.

Sixth point of mediation: QoS/QoP (Quality-of-Service and Quality-of-Protection)

Mediation of QoS/QoP covers a number of related topics all falling under the heading of performance oriented concerns. Taken together, these considerations, dealt with inside the ESB, enable service scaling, response time and availability objectives to be met, along with security and audit requirements, allowing the establishment of SLA (Service- and Security-Level Agreement) to be expressed and enforced in a completely policy- or configuration-driven manner. Absent an ESB, all these complex considerations fall back to the service itself or to point solutions that only deal with one or two of these concerns at a time and do so outside the context of a global management architecture and framework.

QoS specifically breaks down into 5 distinct but highly interrelated issues:
• High availability
• Load distribution
• Routing optimization
• Queuing (asynchronous delivery)
• Publish-and-Subscribe (1:N distribution cardinality, or syndication)

The ESB infrastructure should, and usually does, support some degree of HA architecture that ensures continuity of communications and integrity of message flow between service end-points. The most robust incarnations of these models provide five-nines, 'continuous-availability' of the infrastructure through sophisticated state-full replication between ESB elements, such that any failure of an infrastructure element remains entirely transparent to attached services (i.e., no loss of connection, logon or transaction state). In conjunction with the next two aspects of QoS, this also extends degrees of fault-tolerance and HA to the services themselves.

Regarding route optimization, one can also then consider the earlier example where service developers might be motivated to directly connect two services for pipeline speed between them. If two services needed to be deployed in a way that reduced the message passing latency between services in order to make the entire service orchestration run faster, the optimal architecture would be to place all the services in the same execution container and pass the messages between the services as objects that are not dependent upon the network between each service step. However, if the services needed to be deployed to support maximum scale, handling potentially thousands of simultaneous requests, one might be more inclined to deploy the services across many containers to horizontally scale the application platform. If service designers were forced to decide these options one-way-or-another, and optimize the implementation of the service for either, the service would not be in a position to readily adapt and be reused in the alternate context. If an ESB was used, this decision could be deferred to deployment time, where an operations engineer could determine the appropriate scale and latency for the situation and make policy-driven deployment decisions to support either or both simultaneously.

Over and above speed, scale and latency considerations, quality of service also extends further to include message integrity and durability concerns as well. At its core this amounts to the ESB's ability to provide reliable queuing. Additionally it introduces support for synchronous to asynchronous interaction mediation. For example, if someone wants to ask you a question over the phone in real-time (synchronously) but you are unavailable so they leave you a voice-mail, 'queued' in the persistent storage of your voicemail box which (asynchronously) 'brokers' the question for you. This is a form of 'guaranteed' delivery that mediates sync to async interaction and enables a level of loose coupling (of both time and dialog mode), while still assuring proper delivery, that forms one of the principal drivers for an ESB.

This notion extends one level further when one considers that such interactions are not always one-to-one. Sometimes these capabilities are necessary in multi-party or one-to-N communications. Fundamentally, this is known publish-and-subscribe communications where services can syndicate around information (topics) of interest and receive notifications, as a broadcast, when events occur. One could argue that 1:N cardinality of communications is the most significant driver for ESB usage.

Again however, what makes these notions of particular interest in an ESB is that these performance selections are completely abstracted away from service implementation such that decisions on the level of availability, topological virtualization, load distribution, pipelining, queue reliability (persistence) and cardinality are no longer placed in the service designer's view. With respect to Quality-of-Protection, it is possible, in certain cases, to look at an ESB as a common security assertion, control and enforcement layer for all interactions across the enterprise—a fortress wall that one rings around their service environment to protect it in all interaction circumstances. These security considerations extend to authentication, authorization, audit, encryption, and other related concerns, and purports to enable all these things to be dealt with in a policy-driven, declarative manner as well. In doing so, it establishes one common enforcement point, across firewall, DMZ and domain borders, where all services can be relieved of these considerations and the enterprise can trust that all QoP assertions can be uniformly implemented across all services now, and as new services appear in the future.

Another point of view is that security can only be viewed as a multi-layer problem extending downward from the ESB all the way into the hardware level, and above the ESB all the way up to the application or service layers themselves—in this model the ESB is simply a participant in security contributing some enforcement and surveillance capability but not necessarily addressing the entirety of enterprise security concerns.

Seventh point of mediation: Interaction Model

The final point of mediation has to do with Interaction Model. Services will communicate using one of four possible interaction models: Request/Reply, Pub/Sub, Store-and-Forward (a.k.a. Fire-and-Forget), and Batch Files. Even if there were a day in the future when everything was 100% Web Service compliant, it is still possible that services may not be able to interact. For example, one service chooses WS-ReliableMessaging (the one that supports the store-and-forward and request-reply variants) and another speaks WS-Eventing (a pub/sub variant). Even though both are fully standards compliant, the two would still never interact. This is because one wants to publish events when information changes and the other wants to ask questions when it needs information. Once again, it is impractical to consider that all services can be normalized to interact in one common model. ESBs enable interaction model differences to be delegated to the infrastructure for mediation without writing custom logic. Thus it becomes possible to get two services interacting, despite differences in dialog making the services reusable over a larger range of contexts and more agile to respond to new situations.

Interrelationships Between The Seven Points Of Mediation

Having now reviewed the seven points of mediation individually, it is worth noting one key observation that you may have made along the way: that there is a strong interrelationship between the various points of mediation just described. In each of the examples used to illustrate the discrete points of mediation, there was an implied dependency on one or more of the other forms of mediation. Look for an ESB that encompasses all seven points of mediation in a comprehensive manner and enables all of them to be managed in a coordinated way across all service interactions.

Mediating Toward The Pure Service

The ESB provides a mechanism through which 'pure' services can be created. In other words, services that are created with the correct functional granularity (i.e., not 'over-composited' into a single service, and not so state-full across interactions as to become components) and also delegate fully the seven points of mediation to infrastructure, become reusable across the widest range of circumstances, thereby preserving and reinforcing the SOA logic chain toward agility, Business-IT alignment and faster realization of value from IT investments.

4.6 Conclusion

Interoperability is probably the primary driver for an ESB initiative— establishing a platform to implement and govern a broad range of mediation types in order to bring about interoperability, scalability and manageability of SOA in ways that transcend what standards alone can offer. SOA is first and foremost about heterogeneity—be prepared for it at every level of the SOA. Build a philosophy around Interchangeable, best-of-breed parts. ESB enables that interchangeability so that heterogeneity can be leveraged for best-of-breed capabilities without compromising manageability, reuse or agility.

Over and above the interoperability provided by standards, ESB fills gaps not yet satisfied by state-of-the-art and even enables mediation across incompatible standards. ESB binds the links of the 'SOA-chain of logic' together to ensure that your SOA initiative fully achieves the reuse, agility and business value objectives you seek.

CHAPTER 5

Runtime Management

Paul Butterworth
Chief Technology Officer

AmberPoint

Successful implementation of a SOA initiative includes the creation of a service network consisting of applications and services constructed using an SOA approach. Developers now have several years of experience successfully building such service networks and are reaping the benefits promised by SOA, including decreased development costs and increased agility. However, these experienced developers have also seen that these benefits can be quickly offset by increased operational costs for these complex service networks. To help minimize operational costs while increasing the agility and overall cost-effectiveness of the resulting service network organizations are embracing SOA runtime governance.

You will find SOA runtime governance is most effective if these tasks are addressed in an automated fashion and if its capabilities span a heterogeneous infrastructure on which the service network resides. Coding runtime governance into application components result in constant recoding as the system grows and evolves. For this reason, it is recommended to create an abstracted runtime governance layer, one that accommodates change and thereby fosters system agility.

In this chapter we will address some of the practical issues that arise in the course of performing runtime governance tasks, describe the best practices for addressing issues, and show how runtime governance solutions, when implemented properly, can lead to increased agility and decreased costs.

We will address important considerations, including:

- Understanding service network topology
- Ensuring the operational health of the Service network
  - Managing performance and availability
  - Delivering appropriate service levels
- Detecting and diagnosing exceptions in the behavior of the service network
- Securing the Service network
- Ensuring the integrity of the Service network as it evolves

KEY RECOMMENDATIONS:

There are three overarching runtime governance requirements for SOA. Address these and you will ensure greater operational effectiveness and system agility. Try to do business with SOA systems without having addressed them and you won't get far. These requirements include:

- Understanding the composition and behavior of your service network

- Controlling your service network as well as detecting, diagnosing and, ultimately, preventing problems that arise during the operation of the service network

- Ensuring the correctness of your operational system as it evolves over time

5.1 Understanding Topologies

Service networks can and should be dynamic to allow services to be added, updated or removed at any time. In such a shifting environment, it can be a challenge to understand what is actually installed and running—the 'as-built' structure of the service network as opposed to the intended structure of the service network. We have all been victim to situations where the topology of a system is explained to us by the system's 'authority.' Of course, it's at the worst possible time that we come to find that the system's actual topology is different from what was described. After investigation, we might find the culprit to be a service that nobody knew was part of the system. This problem is common in the SOA world where any service may be added to the topology simply by calling it while there may be no record of the existence of this call.

In this instance you would rely on runtime governance, which solves this problem by dynamically discovering the topology of the service network. It observes the actual components that are installed in the environment—no matter if it exists in a development, staging or production environment—and records their existence. Since these are SOA-based environments and the service interfaces can be accessed dynamically, details of the discovered service's interface can also be recorded. As an added benefit, the runtime governance system can record the discovery information in a registry or repository, making the information available to the architecture, development, and operational teams. We've seen that the most successful IT shops instrument all their service environments used in development, QA and operations. They can then use the information on discovered services as the basis for the overall SOA governance by recording which services exist, their current state, and the rate at which the services are being promoted from one lifecycle stage to another. This information, along with usage information described below, is used to prepare reports for corporate management detailing the effectiveness of their SOA initiatives.

Let's consider another example. In the spring of 2007, daylight savings time changed in the US about a month earlier than usual. The time change required that every service was checked to make sure that appropriate patches had been applied to the systems on which they were hosted. By automatically discovering the services in the environment, the runtime governance system gives us a guarantee that all service environments have been properly updated. If we depend on only design-time information, we'd likely miss services incorporated into the application in the later stages of development or substituted during subsequent maintenance activities or just simply not recorded from the start. One user reported it took only five minutes to discover all affected services and issue change requests to the operation staff to check their environments. The daylight savings change went off without a hitch!

In a similar vein, you will certainly need to know the effects of a component failure, the potential impact of a change to a component or who is using a particular component. In order to answer these questions you first need to know the interdependencies among your application components—another capability you'll derive from your SOA runtime governance system.

A runtime governance solution observes a service's inbound and outbound message traffic to identify other services to which they are connected. As it observes more and more services it constructs a picture of the actual service components that comprise the system and their interconnections. Runtime governance tracks this information across the service network, producing an accurate network connectivity topology based on actual traffic. This results in an authoritative record of the dependencies among services.

This information forms the basis for impact analysis. You can see which components of the service network are likely to be impacted by a change to a service. Generally, impacted components will be in the set of callers of the changed service and/or the set of services the changed service calls. The set of callers should be computed transitively to gain visibility into 'indirect' callers of a service. Given this information, we can determine who will be impacted and can give all interested parties (i.e., the callers) advance warning of the change so they can prepare. Using your runtime governance system you can even take this a step further by recording the set of end users of a particular service. For instance, you can use this information to notify users of outages caused by the failure of a particular service. This is another example of a SOA best practice enabled by runtime governance—taking a proactive approach to work with the user community.

You should be able to leverage this dependency tracking to help document the effectiveness of the SOA program. By recording all uses of the services—both by other services and end users—you can gain a clear picture of actual reuse and the rate of change in reuse throughout the organization. Such information illustrates the effectiveness of the SOA program, highlights the most effective services, and serves as an early warning of reuse problems that might surface. For example, a service may have been built with the expectation of significant reuse. Should we discover that the service is not actually being reused we can initiate further investigation to determine if applications that were expected to reuse the service have instead created independent solutions. This is a good example of something that's usually checked during the early phases of the software development lifecycle, rather than discovering the problem in the operational environment after the application has been deployed. This is another reason for enabling the runtime governance system throughout all lifecycle phases.

5.2 Managing Operational Health

It is essential to manage the operational health of your service network. At its most basic, this requirement boils down to understanding the performance and availability of your service network. You need to know about the performance of both the services and the composite applications that comprise your service network. Once you have control of these basic characteristics of your service network, you can advance to managing the specific service levels provided to the clients.

IT professionals familiar with the operation of traditional systems are familiar with performance and availability management as well as service level management. However, the service network throws a few wrinkles into the problem—issues that must be considered both by the runtime governance system and the IT organization responsible for the service network.

For example, services are reused. That means the load on the services themselves may change independently of applications that use those services. Thus, the performance of each service (component) must be tracked over time and correlated against the known reuse of the service to determine if new uses of the service will prevent it from properly supporting existing applications. To reuse a service it must indicate how long it will take to produce a response. This represents its expected service level. Under unexpectedly heavy loads the service might not meet this constraint. The trick then is to keep the service from overloading. To do this, you need a way to keep the set of clients of a service from demanding more capacity than the service can offer. Alternatively, you would need a way to increase the capacity of the service. Use runtime governance to solve this problem by tracking and limiting service requests to maintain the request load below that required to meet service level agreements or by adding capacity in conjunction with other infrastructure management systems. There are several strategies to consider, including:

- Configure the service such that all users, at their maximum load, can be serviced
- Use historical statistics to determine a reasonable peak load
- Dynamically adjust the limits for each user to reflect the current load

This problem is a bit insidious when you consider the services that prove to be most reusable are the first to experience a problem. To stay ahead of this issue, track changes in reuse rates to determine which services should be monitored most closely.

The runtime governance system also reports detailed information to make the most of service level agreement monitoring and enforcement. You might need to check this information on a per-end-user or per-transaction-type basis or based on even more detailed information about the request being processed, such as the size of the order. The runtime governance system can slice and dice the data in various dimensions, allowing you to inspect the performance statistics from the most useful vantage point.

There is no point in monitoring the performance of a system or setting system service levels if it is delivered in such a state that it cannot meet its stated requirements. Unfortunately, many services are deployed in just such a state because the principles of runtime governance are not applied to the service during development and quality assurance. We strongly recommend applying runtime governance to SOA systems when they are under development. It is certainly not very difficult to instrument them when they are being tested. Applying runtime governance early in the lifecycle will not only focus your teams on performance issues earlier in the cycle, but it will also give you hard data that can be used to measure the system when it is first staged in a pre-production environment.

5.3 Detecting And Diagnosing Exceptions

Discovery is the first step to visibility. Once we know the topology of the service network we need to understand its dynamic behavior. Is it up and running? Is it properly processing business transactions? Is it performing as we expect? Runtime governance should be able to answer, or at least aid in answering, these questions for the technical operations team.

Let's consider a classic problem that's addressed by SOA runtime governance—the 'all green' status indicator scenario. Though these status lights indicate that every component of the system is up and running, end users are complaining that their requests are not being processed or processed incorrectly. This usually occurs when some element of the system is down but its role in the application has yet to be discovered, or perhaps an element is running but is processing requests incorrectly.

A good example is a service that accesses a database. The database has been damaged in some way so the service is returning incorrect answers, causing other components of the system to fail or produce incorrect answers. Although the components are still up and responding, their responses are incorrect.

A related problem is one where the user does not receive an answer or the system is not processing requests. The macro level impact is known but the reason for the failure and the location of the failure is not. In such cases, figuring out what went wrong and where can be a very difficult task. A classic approach for diagnosing these errors is to have each service log capture information about what it sends and receives, as well as some of its internal activities. The technicians responsible for each service then get together and manually trace their way through logs, correlating messages and looking for anomalies. One organization reported they spent more than 14 hours looking for such a problem that impacted only one customer's transactions—all other customer's transactions were processed correctly. After significant effort, they realized that one service had been updated in a minor way but that change had a deleterious effect on transactions whose serial numbers were encoded in a specific format used by only one customer This would have been much easier to find if correlated log information from all the participating services was readily available to the diagnostic team.

Using runtime governance, you can take much of the labor out of this task. Messages can be recorded and correlated automatically. Standard patterns can be detected automatically and queries and inspections can be applied to the correlated messages in an effort to find anomalous behavior. Once a problem is found, the exact location of the problem is known and corrective action can be taken. If the problem is chronic, perhaps due to some physical failure or some recurring logical inconsistency, the runtime governance system can automatically detect failures and initiate corrective actions.

A great example of the benefits of this runtime governance technology is illustrated in its application to various order fallout or transaction failure problems in integrated systems. That's because the behavior of integrated legacy systems are difficult to predict in all possible situations and under all possible stimuli. Automatically correlating messages and using the resulting log information for diagnostic purposes is essential to the proper operation of the system. As each problem is diagnosed, further rules can be added to the exception system to detect similar problems in the future, thereby making the system even more responsive.

5.4 Security

Traditional applications are typically 'tightly-coupled' and secured at the application level. That is, the user signs in to the application using his or her username and password. Once the user has been authenticated, the application itself authorizes the use of its various features

In a service network, this one-to-one model no longer holds. A SOA application consists of an aggregated set of discrete services, each of which is an independent entity that can be reused across multiple applications. Thus, SOA services cannot depend on a single application to implement authentication and authorization policies—each service must be able to perform a range of security processing independently—authentication, authorization, and so on. In the service network each service is responsible for authenticating the identity of requesters and authorizing the use of various capabilities offered by the service.

A service may not be aware of who the ultimate consumer of the service is, and, at the same time each service must share data that may be used in unpredictable ways by other applications involved in the transaction. An intermediary in one transaction may act as a service consumer in another transaction. Those other applications may dynamically 'plug in' to an existing transaction, or may suddenly be accessed by a foreign partner, where the previous week all access was confined to users within the enterprise walls.

Security processing must be placed within every SOA application. However, implementing security processing in every application would obliterate the core value proposition associated with SOA—*agility*. The response to this seeming conundrum is a runtime governance system that simultaneously offloads security processing and policy enforcement from the applications themselves, while enabling embedded security processing on their behalf.

The best practice response to this challenge is to implement authentication and authorization at the service interface. This offloads security programming and configuration from application developers and places responsibility for security in the hands of security administrators. The role of a runtime governance solution is to provide a mechanism for offloading security processing from the services themselves, while decoupling the definition of security policies from their execution in the system. A key challenge is policy enforcement at the service endpoint. This is conventionally known as *'last-mile security.'*

If security processing does not occur locally on the machine where the service is running, inevitably all requests will have to traverse the network for one final hop *after* security processing has taken place. The effect of this is that when an SOA message is at its most vulnerable, an inferior—or even worse — *proprietary* security mechanism is employed. Therefore, the best practice is to deploy a solution that enables embedded last-mile security—policy enforcement at the service endpoint.

This may be implemented as a collaborative effort among the runtime infrastructure components supporting the service network, including runtime governance. Specific security needs that can be met by the runtime governance system working in conjunction with the application infrastructure include:

- Populating messages with user credentials
- Authenticating requesters
- Determining if an authenticated requester is authorized to make a specific request
- Managing privacy and integrity
- Propagating identity information across multiple service invocations

Authentication

Authentication is the process of verifying the identity claimed by a service requester. In an SOA, best practice is for the requester to supply credentials in a WS-Security header that can be authenticated by the service. Two types of credentials are most common in current systems.

- Username/Password Pairs
- X.509 Certificates

Another common approach is to rely on the message traffic being transported over HTTP and using its basic authentication rather than incorporating the credentials into the message. This works as long as the link terminates at the service that processes the request, but if there are intermediate hops in the processing chain the credentials will not reach the ultimate target service. This forces the intermediate processors of the message to either figure out how to propagate HTTP basic credentials from an inbound to an outbound message or to attach their own credentials to the outbound message. However, this creates a traceability problem as we then don't know the identity of the original requestor. The WS-Security model is simpler to use since the credentials can be easily forwarded with subsequent messages.

Authorization

Authentication determines the identity of the service requester. Authorization determines what an authenticated user is allowed to do. Flexible authorization is a critical component of an SOA due to the potential for unintended reuse of services. For example, you may release a service to support your internal administrative users, only to find later that the service is to be included in a composite application exposed to your overseas subsidiary. For example, it may be necessary for regulatory reasons to restrict the operations accessible to users in the subsidiary. Rather than modifying the business logic of the service to account for these new users, the enterprise should rely on a runtime governance system for providing and enforcing flexible access control (authorization) policies to inbound service requests. 'Coarse-grained' authorization policies determine whether the user can access a service holistically. 'Fine-grained' authorization policies specify exact features or 'operations' accessible by a user.

In response to the challenge of unforeseen reuse, it is recommended that fine-grained access control should always be used for SOA services to ensure that users are not capable of exploiting specific features of a service due to broad general policies. Authorization policies usually leverage role-based access control. That is, an authenticated user is associated with one or more *roles*. This is typically accomplished by verifying user credentials against a *user store*, which may be a simple LDAP-compliant directory or be a full-featured *Identity Management System* (IMS.) The user store returns a set of roles associated with the authenticated user. For example, user `jdoe@abc.com` may be in the role `'BusinessUser'`. It is then the job of the runtime governance system to enforce the mapping of the user's role to the features of the service available to users in that role. The runtime governance system should delegate all user and role management to a dedicated IMS solution. The governance system should in turn provide the functionality necessary to leverage the IMS and to perform fine-grained authorization at the service endpoint.

Privacy and Integrity

Privacy and integrity are critical features in SOA, given that SOA services are designed to reflect business processes, which in turn may be covered by a range of regulatory controls—two well-known examples are Sarbanes-Oxley, and the Payment Card Industry Data Security Standard (PCI DSS.)

Privacy means that only authorized users can see the content of the message—this is usually enforced through encryption schemes or content filtering mechanisms. *Integrity* means that the content of the message has not been tampered with—this is usually enforced by including a digital signature in the message.

Runtime governance supports privacy and integrity requirements by implementing XML Signature, XML Encryption and WS-Security.

Encryption is a computationally expensive operation, so privacy is implemented only on the specific elements of the message body—such as social security or credit card numbers—that are sensitive or regulated. The remainder of the message usually remains clear text. For messages transiting public portions of the Internet, SSL is used to ensure the privacy of the overall message. It should be noted that encryption of sensitive elements of the message are still required since SSL is a link-based protocol. Once the message has been received by the SSL endpoint the message reverts to its clear text form.

SOA services are often responsible for transmitting sensitive or regulated data across the network. As an SOA evolves, more and more consumers may come to rely on that data. However, from a governance standpoint, access to that data must be controlled in a way that reflects corporate policy as it relates to the various regulations around data sharing. Censorship policy, or content filtering, ensures that unless a consumer has the appropriate entitlements, sensitive or regulated data never leave the container where the service is running.

5.5 Ensuring Operational Integrity

A key to maintaining the operational integrity of the service network is effectively managing change. One of the great challenges to success with SOA is validating the correct operation of the service network when a change is introduced. The operational integrity problem is amplified in the SOA environment due to the nature of the service network and can have a significant impact in several areas including:

- **Shared Services.** Since services are shared among applications a change to a service may impact many applications. It can be challenging to ensure that all applications that use a service continue to operate correctly after a change.

- **Dynamically Changing Services.** Services may change dynamically since a change to a service is 'effective' as soon as the updated service is installed and message traffic is delivered. Since a service in the operational environment may require a change to support a new or existing application, all applications that use the service may be impacted by the change.

- **Federated Services.** A service might not be owned by a consumer of that service. This means the service may change without notice. It also means a test version of the service may not be available for validating changes to the application. In such an environment, it is difficult to ensure the operational correctness of the application in the face of changes and to develop and test application updates without impacting the operation of the production service.

- **Federated Service Consumers.** The consumers of a service may be federated. Thus, the owners of a service may not have access to the consumers of the service to validate changes made to the service. When the consumers are out of our control it becomes very difficult to ensure the modified service continues to provide proper support.

Runtime governance has introduced facilities for supporting a new discipline – operational validation –developed specifically to address the problem of validating the service network in the face of:

- Continuous and Dynamic Change
- Federated Services and Service Consumers

SOA operational validation facilities are designed to address the unique characteristics of the service network that make validation such a challenge. The validation facilities capture traffic flowing through production environments for use in service validation. They then validate an application (or a system) by submitting captured request messages to the application's services and comparing the results with captured responses to determine whether the application is operating correctly.

Use the runtime governance system for validating both the functional and performance characteristics of the application:

- By capturing interleaved traffic from all consumers of a service the system validates changed services by presenting them with a realistic sampling of the traffic they have to support. This also solves a common problem of the service support team not having access to federated consumers of the service for testing purposes.

- The captured traffic is presented periodically to validate federated services that may change without notification. Thus, the operations team has increased assurance that the services they consume continue to behave as expected.

- The captured traffic is presented each time a service is known to change. Thus, dynamic changes in the operational environment can be validated.

- The captured traffic also forms the basis of service simulators used for testing new applications against federated services for which native test facilities have not been made available.

5.6 Conclusion

Runtime governance plays a vital role in any SOA system. Not only does it reduce costs and increase operational effectiveness, it ensures that applications perform as expected and withstand changes as the service network evolves.

It's important to remember that there's more to runtime governance than simply monitoring the service network. You must be able to control the system and its components as well. Monitoring without control is like a police force that watch crimes take place but do nothing about them. To bring reliability to SOA applications, runtime governance must not only detect issues, it must also resolve them before these problems can affect the business.

Due to the number of moving parts in a SOA environment, it's not a scalable solution to rely on manual effort to handle runtime governance tasks. Wherever possible, automate your runtime governance to achieve greater effectiveness and minimize the chances of human error. Your runtime governance solution must span a heterogeneous infrastructure on which the service network resides, so it is important to look for a solution that's well integrated with leading application servers, enterprise service buses and other SOA infrastructure. Close vendor partnerships in this industry can take some of the bumps out of your SOA adoption path.

With a runtime governance system that provides visibility into and automated control of your complete services network, you'll be better prepared to reap the benefits of SOA.

CHAPTER 6

Organizing For Success

Hemant Ramachandra
Managing Director,
Business Systems Integration

BearingPoint

In the early 2000s, a large multinational electronics manufacturer began building Web services as part of a strategic enterprise-wide commitment to SOA. In many ways, the initiative was successful: Multiple divisions throughout the company together created hundreds of robust services that addressed very real business needs. However, although the SOA mandate came from the top of the organization, there was no attempt to set up a central governance mechanism to monitor, control, and coordinate the proliferation of services throughout the company. As a result, although many of the services met the functional requirements of individual divisions, they were too narrowly focused to be easily discovered and reused by others. Developers from different businesses developed overlapping or redundant services. And even when a service was shared across divisions, each one would alter it to solve its particular needs, thus making it difficult to reuse elsewhere. Despite the promise of SOA, the hoped-for return on investment (ROI) has not yet materialized.

This firm is not alone in struggling organizationally with SOA despite commendable technical achievements. Indeed, the challenges it faces are common to most companies who have moved past initial pilot projects that experiment with Web services to more ambitious company-wide SOA initiatives.

SOA has unique organizational challenges when compared to other strategic IT or business initiatives. It requires a rather schizophrenic mindset: After all, the ability to set and implement business and technical initiatives that span multiple organizational boundaries has long been—and should be—the purview of senior management. Yet for SOA to provide sustainable value, individual lines of businesses, departments, or even workgroups must be empowered to create services that have the potential to impact the entire enterprise without getting higher-ups involved.

Your ability to reconcile these seemingly contradictory organizational mandates—in which a highly structured vision of your company's business and technological future facilitates a decentralized explosion of creative development activities—will determine the success of your SOA strategy.

KEY RECOMMENDATIONS:

- Establish and enforce architectural standards and guidelines.

- Set up and empower centralized groups to enforce governance and evolve them as needed.

- Recruit and/or train personnel with the appropriate skill sets.

- Leverage an effective capacity-planning mechanism.

- Create an appropriate funding model.

- Draw up well-defined guidelines for identifying, modeling, implementing, discovering, consuming, and deploying services.

- Implement a portfolio of service-management capabilities.

- Align your software development lifecycle (SDLC) processes with your SOA efforts.

6.1 Key SOA Success Factors

Indeed, whether your SOA initiatives fly or fail depend on your ability to institute a robust governance function that maintains control over all SOA-related activities throughout the enterprise. Among other things, a centralized approach to governance will allow you to:

- **Establish and enforce architectural standards and guidelines.** A successful SOA strategy requires strict adherence to a reference architecture that has been planned, designed, and documented with cross-organizational reuse of services in mind.

- **Set up and empower centralized groups to enforce governance and evolve them as needed.** New organizational structures are needed to keep different lines of business, departments, or workgroups in compliance with mandated architectural and business process standards. But these structures must be flexible enough to grow and change as your business does.

- **Recruit and/or train personnel with the appropriate skill sets.** One of the chief challenges facing companies wishing to implement SOA is finding business and technical professionals capable of implementing the SOA vision. One common solution is to hire outside consultants who possess the necessary expertise; however, it's critical to institute a process for transferring key skills and knowledge to internal workers from Day One.

- **Leverage an effective capacity-planning mechanism.** Once you begin developing services, you might be surprised how quickly they proliferate. Such services can easily eat up systems as well as personnel resources, and you must be constantly monitoring their use and growth so as to allocate sufficient resources to the right people and projects.

- **Create an appropriate funding model.** It actually costs more initially to develop a service that can be reused across an organization than to build one that meets a particular business need. Organizations must provide funding that supplements SOA development efforts by individual groups— or finds some way to share costs across them—so as not to overburden any one stakeholder with the cost of developing services that will be used throughout the enterprise.

- **Draw up well-defined guidelines for identifying, modeling, implementing, discovering, consuming, and deploying services.** Without having this mandated by a centralized authority, there will be no consistency about how services developed by various internal groups are conceived of, developed, and implemented, and the opportunity for reuse—and therefore ROI—will be greatly diminished.

- **Implement a portfolio of service-management capabilities.** This includes service registration, publishing and provisioning; service versioning; service monitoring; service auditing; service publishing; and service security.

- **Align your software development lifecycle (SDLC) processes with your SOA efforts.** Again, this is best done by a centralized authority that can facilitate consistency across all organizational units.

6.2 Using A SOA Maturity Model To Facilitate Business And IT Alignment

SOA initiatives have a greater chance of achieving expectations when the focus is on business outcomes rather than technology. Yet making this shift in perspective is often the most difficult part of implementing SOA.

A business-focused SOA approach isolates the technology portion of a service from the business portion and engineers it so that the technology is available to all business processes no matter where they exist in the enterprise. This modular approach to defining business services results in an IT infrastructure that's much more flexible and better aligned with business priorities. And because each SOA project is tied to a business outcome, it's easier to measure success.

Organizationally, this means that you must be careful to put safeguards in place that prevent wasted time and effort. After all, the point is not to create hundreds or even thousands of services and hope that some of them are relevant to and reusable within your business. Rather, the goal is to identify your company's key business processes, detach them from their existing technology implementations, and build independent modules that are immediately—even urgently—relevant to your organization as a whole.

SOA governance is a critical aspect at each stage in the SOA maturity module.

- **Level 1: Initial Services.** When embarking on SOA, companies need to establish IT architectural leadership. They also must begin institutionalizing the use of SOA concepts for developing or modifying enterprise applications. Organizations that establish a clear overall vision are taking their first step toward achieving business benefits.

- **Level 2: Architected Services.** At this level, you begin to create partnerships between business and technology stakeholders for SOA governance. IT also needs to extend SOA processes to business units to facilitate collaboration on improving business processes. You should be able to begin calculating the ROI derived from business-related activities at this point.

- **Level 3: Business and Collaborative Services.** Once SOA-architected services have been implemented, you must continue deepening the partnerships between business and technology units in order to meet governance mandates. Additionally, you should begin to support full business processes via SOA, and should be able to prove significant ROI from your ability to both reuse services and rapidly respond to changes in the business environment.

- **Level 4: Measured Business Services.** At this stage, you can finally effect a transformation from reactive to real-time business processes. By defining and meeting business-oriented performance metrics, you can measure ROI based on SOA's positive impact on the business.

- **Level 5: Continuously Improving Business Services.** Finally, when you reach this level you must implement enterprise-wide leadership processes that align business initiatives with the SOA strategy. At this point, ROI will depend on your ability to support continuous improvement while meeting the organization's overall strategic goals.

6.3 Laying The Organizational Groundwork

One of the biggest myths of SOA is that you should start small and create it on the fly. Start small, yes. But without a strategic vision, you could end up like the firm with the hundreds of individual services and no ROI in sight.

Here are three 'due diligence' steps you should take in preparation for beginning your SOA endeavor:

Step One: Create a strong statement of SOA vision

This overarching statement must answer the question: "Why SOA?" from the point of view of the various constituencies to facilitate buy in at the executive level, by the various business units, and by IT professionals.

This statement should include details of how SOA projects will be funded, and what sort of processes will be put into place so that services have a good chance of being discovered and reused throughout the organization.

The vision should also include a description of the reference architecture that draws from existing technical components available in the legacy environment.

The vision statement should also provide the basic framework for governance and begin laying the groundwork for an enterprisewide SOA center of excellence.

You should also think of your vision statement as the foundation for your SOA evangelism activities that you should jump start fairly early in the SOA process. Some starting points to make as you prepare to 'sell' your vision include:

- **Executive leadership.** Senior managers are most interested in the organizational agility and competitive advantages promised by SOA.

- **Business users.** You will get their attention by emphasizing the reduced costs, decreased time to market, and enhanced quality of service that SOA can deliver.

- **IT management.** In addition to the above-mentioned benefits that accrue to business users, IT managers will be most interested in hearing how SOA has the potential for transforming the current monolithic and rigid IT model to one that is modular, flexible, and which can quickly adopt to meet the changing needs of the business.

- **Development/data architects.** By introducing them to the new standards-based technologies that result in a 'cleaner' architecture that facilitates easier integration, they'll get on board more quickly.

- **Operations/Support.** These professionals will be interested in how SOA provides consistency in the way applications are built and deployed that will make them easier to manage, maintain, and monitor.

Step Two: Customize the vision

Next, you need to hone in further to understand the specific needs of each group of stakeholders as it relates to the current state of the systems infrastructure.

This statement should include an explanation of your firm's change-management strategy and how it will be implemented, as well as identify the constraints—both technical and organizational—that stand in the way of SOA adoption. It's important to keep in mind that few organizations readily embrace wholesale change, and your SOA vision must take this into account. The pace of adoption you set must be realistic, and the steps small and discrete enough to increase the probability that you will succeed.

Step Three: Identify potential early adopters

By closely partnering with internal groups that understand the concept of service orientation, you will more quickly deliver results that act as proofs-of-concept that will convince other groups of the validity of your SOA strategy. You can do this in a variety of ways. Often organizations already have 'liaison' or solutions groups within IT whose job it is to identify opportunities for using technology to reduce costs, enhance operational efficiency or even generate additional revenues. Certain business groups can be identified as good candidates for initial SOA projects because robust industry standards have already been established—as in financial services—and it's easy to begin thinking about standardizing both data and processes at various levels in the technology stack.

Other ways to identify potential early adopters include

- Identifying business units at higher maturity levels (assuming SOA assessment is done already)
- Identifying the business units that will benefit the most from SOA
- Identifying less complex business units for SOA enablement to restrict scope and demonstrate early successes

6.4 Establishing Basic Organizational Structures

After performing your preliminary due diligence, you should begin designing and building the necessary governance structures that will make it possible to empower decentralized development of services while helping guard against 'rogue' initiatives by individual groups. Depending on what governance structures you already have in place—for example, you may already have a strong IT project management office—you may decide to leverage existing organizations rather than set up new ones.

There are various benefits and challenges to setting up these structures, however. For example, many organizations set up a common services group to develop, deploy and manage common reusable services across the enterprise. Although this is a good practice, some companies don't understand the skill set required for such a group—which includes business savvy and top-notch communications abilities in addition to technical prowess—thus making them bottlenecks rather than successful facilitators of SOA. And it's essential that all of the governance bodies should be headed by director-level managers to ensure the right degree of commitment to create the needed processes as well as systems within required timeframes.

The Project Management Office (PMO)

This group should enforce rigorous governance over financial budgets as well as delivery timeframes. By being very specific about the required SDLC, compliance metrics, and exception processes that SOA projects must conform to, the PMO becomes the central controlling mechanism for completing SOA projects on time and within budget. Among other things, the PMO should be responsible for determining exactly where in the delivery lifecycle the architecture review board should take action, and should report directly to the CIO.

Staffing a PMO for SOA requires somewhat different skill sets than a traditional IT PMO.

Center of Excellence

Also known as the enterprise architecture (EA) Group, this organization should enforce technology compliance against a well-documented organizational blueprint and set of architectural principles. The center of excellence should report directly to the CTO and has responsibility for achieving strict compliance, service reuse, and budgetary goals as well as for establishing key architectural standards, guidelines, principles, and recommendations. And if the center of excellence is not involved early in the SOA process, you might not effectively mitigate all the technological and financial risks.

In addition to evangelizing the SOA vision, the center of excellence defines how standards will be adopted throughout the enterprise. It defines and publishes the architecture principles of the SOA reference architecture as well as details on how those should be implemented, and often provides the technical subject matter expertise. Indeed, the center frequently acts as an internal consulting organization so that experience and knowledge gained by one development effort is shared across the enterprise.

Certainly this center must be staffed with technical experts. But those people must also have a process-centric viewpoint, possess the ability to understand business requirements, and understand how to translate complex technical concepts into language non-technologists can readily understand.

The Change Control Board (CCB)

This should be environment- or function- specific and should confirm proper procedures have been followed prior to release of any software into the production environment

The professionals on this board must understand enough about the business needs as well as culture of individual departments or divisions to establish realistic guidelines for discovering and modifying services. By controlling changes to either the data or the services, this prevents individual users from making alterations that preclude others within the organization from using the services or data.

6.5 Implementing The Proper Service Discovery Model

For your SOA center of excellence to be effective, it must meet three key requirements. First, it must have a good understanding of the requirements of multiple internal customers. Next, it must possess a strong sense of how much you will need to invest up front in a service to make it universally reusable. Finally, it must establish an effective governance structure to manage the reuse of any services created.

To succeed at all this, the SOA center of excellence must implement a 'service discovery model' that provides a layered view of technology assets to support the business, and which provides a visual depiction of your ability to reuse services across various lines of business (see Figure 6.1).

- **Business Capabilities View.** Your SOA center of excellence must first create a view that establishes high-level requirements that are aligned with your organizations overarching strategic vision.

- **Business Services View.** Then, your center of excellence must be able to identify process commonalities across businesses and begin to define services that can support those processes across organizational boundaries.

- **Technical Component View.** After that, the center of excellence lays out the technical components that support the business service view.

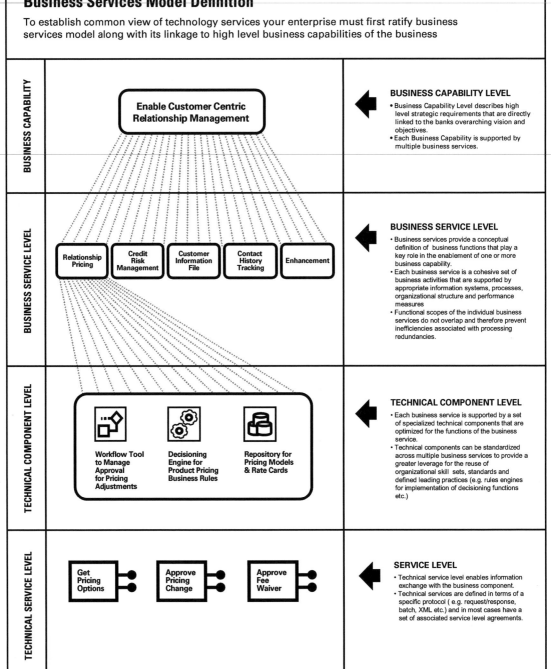

Business Services Model Definition

To establish common view of technology services your enterprise must first ratify business services model along with its linkage to high level business capabilities of the business

BUSINESS CAPABILITY

Enable Customer Centric Relationship Management

BUSINESS CAPABILITY LEVEL
- Business Capability Level describes high level strategic requirements that are directly linked to the banks overarching vision and objectives.
- Each Business Capability is supported by multiple business services.

BUSINESS SERVICE LEVEL

| Relationship Pricing | Credit Risk Management | Customer Information File | Contact History Tracking | Enhancement |

BUSINESS SERVICE LEVEL
- Business services provide a conceptual definition of business functions that play a key role in the enablement of one or more business capability.
- Each business service is a cohesive set of business activities that are supported by appropriate information systems, processes, organizational structure and performance measures
- Functional scopes of the individual business services do not overlap and therefore prevent inefficiencies associated with processing redundancies.

TECHNICAL COMPONENT LEVEL

Workflow Tool to Manage Approval for Pricing Adjustments

Decisioning Engine for Product Pricing Business Rules

Repository for Pricing Models & Rate Cards

TECHNICAL COMPONENT LEVEL
- Each business service is supported by a set of specialized technical components that are optimized for the functions of the business service.
- Technical components can be standardized across multiple business services to provide a greater leverage for the reuse of organizational skill sets, standards and defined leading practices (e.g. rules engines for implementation of decisioning functions etc.)

TECHNICAL SERVICE LEVEL

Get Pricing Options

Approve Pricing Change

Approve Fee Waiver

SERVICE LEVEL
- Technical service level enables information exchange with the business component.
- Technical services are defined in terms of a specific protocol (e.g. request/response, batch, XML etc.) and in most cases have a set of associated service level agreements.

- **Technical Service View.** Finally, you specify how the technical services and associated technology assets will support both the enterprise business view and business service view.

By progressively drilling down in the views, you are able to identify opportunities for reuse across high-level business needs. By leveraging your SOA center of excellence to do this, you end up with a number of candidates for services that have a high probability of being reused—and therefore increase your chance of recouping your investment.

Once the initial set of projects has been identified, the SOA center of excellence group takes responsibility for refining them further based on detailed analyses of additional factors including your organization's ability to reuse the services in question; the complexity of the services in terms of implementation, governance, deployment, monitoring, and management; and balancing the tactical versus strategic business and technical objectives

6.6 Creating A SOA Roadmap

An executable SOA roadmap has two principle attributes: It actively manages the risks associated with the success and growth of the program; and it clearly delineates the financial value to each of the constituents.

Organizationally, a SOA roadmap has both an enterprise dimension and an LOB dimension. The LOB determines the build out and the sequencing and the pace of adoption while the enterprise manages the risks associated with the development of common services.

Financially, funding support should be provided by both the enterprise and the LOB. Although the LOB will bear some of the expenses for developing a service, the corporate entity must take a portfolio approach to keep different projects in sync and make sure that there will be sufficient ROI.

Organizationally, it's critical that each of the phases of the roadmap (see Figure 6.2) involves close collaboration between the SOA center of excellence, the business unit sponsoring development of the service, and the actual project team building the service.

A SOA roadmap is executable when each of the stages provide quantifiable value to all constituents. To achieve that result, the roadmap is driven both by business opportunity and technology dependencies. The structures, processes, and procedures are incrementally added as the aggregate number of manageable services grows. Typically at the second or third logical phase of the roadmap is where you begin to see significant business value begin to accrue, because although building a service that is meant to be reusable is more costly, the next time that service is used will generally start accruing some value. As with CMM, few companies venture to the fourth or fifth phase entirely, but instead selectively implement characteristics of each one.

PHASE	DESCRIPTION	EXIT
PHASE 1	1. Establish the governance to enforce the SOA vision (define the vision itself, its principles, and heuristics) 2. Create a staffing/training plan 3. Begin SOA campaign to evangelize SOA throughout the organization 4. Determine funding model 5. Define SOA selection criteria	1. Established governance body 2. Staffing plan 3. SOA communication plan 4. Working funding model 5. Selection criteria
PHASE 2	1. Instrument the governance process and tighten metrics 2. Define, use, and monitor ROI methods 3. Begin implementation of enterprise SOA components (security, continuity, integration) 4. Begin construction of initial services 5. Expansion of effort to include multiple LOBs	1. Governance body executing against metrics 2. ROI models and instances of achieved ROI 3. Infrastructure planning and procurement 4. 3-5 Reusable services 5. Multiple LOB involvement
PHASE 3	1. Introduce governance tools which enforce and monitor standards at the development level 2. Begin metadata management 3. Begin service lifecycle management 4. Introduce business process modeling 5. Begin business domain object construction 6. Begin the design of the data infrastructure	1. Automation of tactical governance 2. Meta data and lifecycle management 3. Business process management (BPM) introduction and service usage strategy 4. 4 well defined canonical objects 5. Data infrastructure design and impact analysis
PHASE 4	1. Introduction and usage of BPM and rules support 2. Construction of dashboards to monitor KPIs 3. Overlay messaging, eventing, and complex event management within the SOA framework	1. Definition and usage of key performance indicators (KPIs) 2. Instrumentation of advanced operational environment 3. Design and implementation of complex event handling
PHASE 5	1. Complete lifecycle control 2. Complete metadata management 3. Focus on continued and measured reuse 4. Complete versioning strategy 5. Full operational control	Continuous improvement phase

You need to consider the following organizational dimensions when constructing the roadmap:

- **Business vision and strategy.** This is the high-level business vision that articulates how your organization plans to improve its current business processes to meet the evolving consumer and market demand.

- **Business value vision.** This is a blended score of opportunities to increase revenues and reduce both costs and overall organizational risk.

- **Technology vision.** This encompasses the set of tools, frameworks, products, and development capabilities that are needed to realize the business vision.

- **Technical viability.** This is the sequence and ability to construct the services which support the business value.

- **Tactical and strategic initiatives.** These are initiatives that need to be completed due to specific needs of the organization. For example, you would typically define compliance-related initiatives at this point.

- **Program progress.** This is the heuristic requirement for building common infrastructure or processes based on the size of the program.

By leveraging the project selection methodology described earlier to identify a candidate list of SOA projects, you should have the organizational structure in place to prioritize the list and perform the following tasks.

- Assess SOA maturity within the organization.
- Determine business risk of implementing SOA.
- Put governance structures in place to address SOA initiatives.
- Determine the business capabilities that need to be delivered to address business requirements.
- Ascertain the level of effort associated with delivering the project.
- Calculate the impacts to existing systems within the enterprise.
- Identify the dependencies associated with the delivery of the projects.
- Put the tools and technologies in place to enable an effective roll-out.
- Determine whether you have the right skill set of IT, business, and operations personnel to build, deploy, manage, and monitor the projects.
- Identify those areas of exception that need to be addressed for compliance reasons.

6.7 Aligning Project Development Processes

Finally, you need to make sure that the organizational framework is in place to monitor and manage the actual development of projects. In particular, this means adjusting your application development methodology to account for SOA-specific skills, responsibilities, and structures.

Requirements
- Business service definition and gap analysis
- Harvesting existing functionality that can be exposed as services
- Non-functional requirements (i.e., performance, scalability, maintainability, manageability)
- Specify service policies, service security and compliance requirements

Dependencies
- For emerging standards, principles, and structure
- Business domain teams to satisfy business goals

Design
- Design of services that comply with client standards
- Review and Sign-Off

Build and Test
- Construction of services in an iterative manner
- Management of the core development to be done in the product
- Unit, system, integration, and performance testing
- Support of 'end-to-end' testing and test automation

Deploy
- Deploy the services in production
- Register the services for enterprise-wide discoverability

Operate
- Monitor services for continuous operation within SLA limits
- Monitor and manage services for policy and compliance

6.8 Conclusion

In summary, your SOA initiative should organizationally be viewed as an enterprise initiative with a significantly broader audience than a departmental one would warrant. This requires putting robust structures in place. Although SOA might seem conceptually simple from an organizational perspective—and its value reasonably self-evident—the implementation challenges can be quite difficult if not planned and executed carefully from an organizational perspective. By putting the framework in place to implement SOA in an evolutionary manner through incremental development and deployment of business applications and reuse of business components, you have a much better chance of building the right architecture and adopting the best practices needed to achieve a shared services vision that facilitates both short- and long-term SOA success.

CHAPTER 7

Capability Development

Jeff Schneider
Chief Executive Officer

MomentumSI

SOA has the ability to transform Information Technology into a more business driven organization. However, change doesn't come easy. In addition to organizational design, process instilment, governance and technology changes, SOA requires a modification in skills and habits.

Service Orientation cuts through virtually all aspects of IT affecting how individuals to do their own job, as well as how they interact with others. Industry analysts such as Gartner have been quick to point out that SOA is less about the technology and more about the change in work processes. Workforces require more than just new tools; they need practical guidance on how their jobs will change on a daily basis. This requires a commitment to training and mentoring to enable the shift. SOA Capability Development and the associated Change Management are fundamental to transforming an organization.

7.1 Getting Started

Figure 7.1: Capability Development Framework

There is no one right way to implement SOA. Many have already traveled the paths before you and have both hit and removed obstacles. The most successful organizations used a structured framework for educating their workforce. (see Figure 7.1)

Skills Assessment

Where are you at today? IT departments vary significantly in their understanding of SOA. The first step to planning the journey is to know where you are starting from. A skills assessment is an easy way to survey the IT organization on their knowledge of general SOA concepts, as well as more in-depth topics related to their specialty area.

> **KEY RECOMMENDATIONS:**
>
> - Start with a skills assessment of where you are today.
>
> - Develop a training roadmap that integrates with your SOA strategy.
>
> - Tailor training by role to maximize individual and organizational effectiveness.
>
> - Tailor the training to your environment.
>
> - Leverage training providers to accelerate adoption.
>
> - Complement training with change management to ensure new skills are utilized.

Most SOA Training providers, will have a method for quickly determining the level of skills maturity in an organization. This typically involves a select few interviews with individuals in various roles, asking questions related to core SOA concepts and techniques.

There are two primary objectives related to the Skills Assessment. First, the assessment determines group strengths and weaknesses so that the training material can be customized to best meet the needs of the class. Second, the assessment is often used as a baseline for measuring the growth of the organization. In this scenario, skills of sample students are tested at both the beginning and end of the program to identify the level of knowledge that has been gained. Additionally, gaps that may remain can be identified.

The Capability Development Roadmap

Where do you want to go? The Capability Development Roadmap is the action plan that enables an organization to move from an 'as-is' to a 'to-be' skills state. The roadmap acts as a constant reminder that SOA isn't just about 'buying a registry' or 'implementing Web Services', but rather a holistic change in how individuals approach their job.

As IT organizations put together their SOA Strategy and Roadmap documents, they define the fundamental reasons why they are doing SOA, as well as the steps that are necessary to achieve their goals. The Capability Development Roadmap is an essential element of the 'SOA Strategy & Roadmap' and should align accordingly.

Most SOA Roadmaps call out several parallel activities, including: Organizational Redesign, Infrastructure Enhancements, SOA Governance, Service Lifecycle Enablement and Capability Development. As these items may run in parallel, it is important to note that capability development, or skills transfer, is usually a prerequisite to performing tasks in the other parallel work-streams. Thus, it is essential to plan training in advance of the other activities.

7.2 Role Based Training

The majority of organizations who have ventured down the SOA path have chosen to perform 'role based' training for their staff. This allows individuals with similar jobs to experience the same training and advice about how to improve their job function. And although no two organizations are alike, a set of job titles has emerged as being core to instilling SOA in an organization. This set includes, but is not limited to CIOs, IT Executives, Business / IT Liaisons, IT Application Owners / Managers, Enterprise Architects, Data Architects, Solutions Architects, Project Managers, Business / Process Analysts, Software Developers, Quality Assurance Professionals, SOA Infrastructure Specialists and Operations Specialists.

CIO / IT Executive

IT leaders have been bombarded with the vendor's view of SOA. While analysts and the press have attempted to clarify the situation, many IT leaders have been given erroneous information. Executive education should focus on the benefits, strategy, costs, risks and timeline. Demonstrations of new technologies or advanced architectures may help bring light to the topic, but should not be a focal point. The primary emphasis should be placed on aligning their understanding of what SOA is, with the rest of the organization. Brief workshops directed at a specific aspect of SOA are an excellent method to accomplish this objective. Virtually all CIO's are time constrained and are unable or unwilling to attend a traditional classroom setting. Consider complementing the workshops with one-on-one sessions between the CIO and the local SOA champion(s). Remember – getting the IT executive leadership educated and on-board with the program is an essential step!

IT Manager

As the IT Executive Leadership becomes more educated on SOA, they will request more information from their staff. Line managers must have a broad understanding of SOA. It should incorporate a deep understanding of how their staff will be applying SOA concepts as well as how activities will change within their peer organizations. IT Managers are encouraged to attend training along with their staff in their domain (architecture, analysis, QA, etc.). In addition, they are encouraged to take training that provides a more in-depth view of SOA. Consider this more of a 'survey course', enabling them to understand the big picture.

Enterprise Architect

IT analysts, such as the Burton Group, have been quick to point out that SOA is first and foremost, an enterprise architecture discipline. Service oriented practitioners agree that the 'service' is the new unit of planning and management in an EA framework. The same practitioners will also note that SOA reference architectures, policies and guidance are essential to a successful program. This said, it is strongly recommend that EA's focus in two areas. The first is related to the overarching infrastructure changes are required to take place. This includes education on modern SOA registries, intermediaries, repositories, orchestration engines, etc. Related to this, the EA should begin to grow their knowledge in how these elements work together to create a united SOA reference architecture. The second area is related to managing groups of services within a domain (Customer Domain, Product Domain, etc.) A new key activity played by the EA is that of 'Enterprise Service Architect'. Here, the individual is taught how to think of the organization as a 'set of services' (not just organizations or functions) and how to identify, and plan the actual realization of these services.

Solution / Application Architect

To date, most solution architects have been taught to think in terms of their solution only. Some might say that today's solution architecture most closely resembles 'Silo Oriented Architecture'. Solution architects must be retrained to view their systems as a set of reusable assets, rather than a stand-alone system. Modern systems are being redesigned into a more loosely coupled structure, where distributed services are the new unit of work. Recombining these services into a 'composite application' rests on the shoulders of the solution architect. Their training should focus on both the decomposition of a system into reusable assets, along with the re-composition of assets into fully functional integrated systems. This involves training in 'Service Design' as well as 'Composite Application Development'.

Data Architect

Data Architects and Information Engineers are perhaps some of the most well equipped people to understand the value and impact of a SOA program. These individuals have experience in many of the areas that others lack such as creating shared services, governing changes to shared services, managing metadata and operating mission critical operational environments. However, these people are most likely not aware of how their canonical models and metadata systems need to be shared with other IT organizations. Their systems and methods will need to be upgraded to adhere to new corporate SOA standards for data delivery, security, transactional integrity and a host of other issues. In addition, more emphasis will be placed on their organizations to deliver a single-source of truth (MDM, CDI, etc.) and to deliver more sophisticated real time access to distributed data sets as a service (EII, federated data queries, etc.) Training for data architects should include modern techniques for data quality, integration and distribution.

Business & Process Analyst

Business and Process Analysts will be the core link between the needs of the business and the IT delivery units. Core to successful Service Oriented Analysis is the decomposition of the business as a set of processes and discrete activities. Modern SOA methodologies require process diagrams as input to identifying and describing services. Failure to perform this analysis may lead to more silo-oriented solutions. It has been said that "silo oriented requirements generate silo oriented solutions." Analysts must be trained to think in terms of shared services, and to actively identify those services in the analysis process. Training sessions should focus on 'Process Modeling for SOA' and should also include lessons on the companies 'Service Oriented Analysis' method.

Software Developer

Many Software Developers think that SOA = Web Services. The first item that needs to be addressed with this group is to reeducate them on what SOA is and is not. They must be shown that the organization is moving to a model where assets are planned, shared and evolved. It is often difficult for software engineers to adjust to the concept of 'building a piece of the solution' rather than 'building the whole solution'. In fact, some software developers may never make the transition. The second item of attention is teaching them how to go about building the services. Most developers specialize in a platform or language like Java or .Net. These platforms have special API's to provide Web Services or RESTful interactions. The developer must also grow a strong understanding of XML, service interfaces and mapping service interfaces back to objects. Last but not least, the developer must understand new techniques for unit testing their system as well as building and deploying their systems along service boundaries.

QA Professional

Quality Assurance professionals will inherit a new breed of systems to validate and verify. These individuals will immediately be challenged by two fundamental changes. First, services are designed to meet the needs of unintended users. That is to say, they are designed to be abstract enough for new consumers to use them with no changes. This presents a challenge to QA groups who are often used to testing systems for very specific use cases. Secondly, the systems which are delivered will be loosely coupled, distributed and potentially built on heterogeneous platforms. Many QA professionals only recently mastered the task of GUI testing and server side load testing. Composite applications and the services that they use present a similar challenge but will take the complexity to a new level. Training should focus on testing individual services (load, functional, security, etc.) as well as on testing the new distributed Composite Applications (integration, performance, etc.)

New SOA Specific Roles

In addition to the roles previously mentioned, many organizations have created new roles that are specific to service orientation. Two that are commonly found are the SOA Infrastructure Specialist and SOA Governance Manager.

SOA Infrastructure Specialist

The SOA Infrastructure Specialist is a technical individual who acts as the primary point of contact for issues relating to the SOA infrastructure (registries, intermediaries, monitors, etc.) This function typically requires deep knowledge in each of the infrastructure areas as well as an ability to integrate disparate areas. Training for this person is a combination of SOA Architecture as well as deep-dive training on each of the products in the environment. It is likely that this person will also provide consulting and informal training to other members of the IT community.

SOA Governance Manager

The SOA Governance Manager is a master planner, manager and negotiator. Their role is multifaceted, requiring a solid understanding of the business and IT In many ways they act as a human intermediary – bringing together services and consumers. They must bridge the gap between service projects and consuming applications. They must also work with enterprise architects to understand the pipeline of new services that are going to be created and the standards, policies and guidelines needed to ensure consistency across the enterprise. The SOA Governance Manager must have fairly deep knowledge in all aspects of SOA and will often training sessions across each area.

7.3 Tailoring The Curriculum To Your Environment

I have created extensive SOA training programs for the enterprise. However, each enterprise has slightly different requirements. It is often necessary to lay the SOA training foundation leveraging a specialist provider for the first 90% and to tailor the last 10% toward your unique environment.

Tailored content typically focuses on decisions that you have made internally that you want to communicate to the department. This might include specific policies for designing services, the use of one protocol over another or how to use internal templates for service analysis. It is often useful to deliver 'bonus material' on your specific environment either during training sessions or as a post-training supplement. As an example, some organizations will train their staff on the general concepts of a SOA registry, taxonomy, etc. Then, they will go to a Web browser and pull up their specific instance of the registry showing the user's important things like how to access it, how to get an account, who to call if they have issues, etc.

Computer Based Training

Many SOA consultancies and training providers now have the more basic courses available as on-demand computer based training (CBT) modules. Although these sessions aren't usually as fulfilling as having a live instructor, they are good in a pinch when remote students can't make the journey or when new employees are on-boarded and need to be brought up to speed.

Interactive Workshops

Often training isn't enough. Workshops are a great way to have a more collaborative exchange of ideas with coworkers. People who have attended classroom training may have grasped the concepts but have a hard time applying it to their job. Workshop sessions are most successful when they are pre-planned, facilitated and have a structured set of exercises for the attendees to work through. Sessions that are popular include "Understanding SOA Governance", "Building a SOA Roadmap" and "Service Investigation and Planning". The duration of these sessions is typically anywhere from a half day to two full days.

Workshops can also be useful when stall-outs occur. This is when a group of people go back to their old habits. Remember, instilling service oriented concepts takes time and effort. SOA program leaders have to be on the lookout for this. It is recommended that you don't chastise those who fall on old habits, but rather work with them to remember the new way of doing things. Often, the people aren't intentionally doing it incorrectly, they just forgot about the new way.

7.4 Change Management

You can lead a horse to water… but you can't make him drink. SOA program leaders have the responsibility to empower the workforce with tools, processes and skills. However, some people will continue to resist any kind of change. As mentioned earlier, it is encouraged that you to work with troubled groups or individuals to understand the importance of this effort and what is expected out of them.

In addition to training, some organizations have created internal SOA forums for discussion, portals of SOA community knowledge and have even created SOA user groups. All of these efforts are often necessary to demonstrate a commitment to the program so that individual contributors don't feel like it's just another passing fad of management.

A growing number of organizations have chosen to use a change management framework to increase the chances of success in their program. The Harvard Business Review recently introduced the 'DICE' method (Duration, Integrity, Commitment, Effort) as a template framework. From a 'Duration' perspective, they noted that a long project that is reviewed frequently is more likely to succeed than a short project that is reviewed infrequently. Capability development goes hand-in-hand with on the job training. Efforts must be planned for active learning session. From an 'Integrity' perspective, organizations look at leaders to ensure that they are providing the resources and runway necessary to succeed. It ensures they are not just getting lip-service. This leads to 'Commitment'. Are the leaders truly backing the initiative? Are they regularly expressing the importance of the effort? Is the message convincing? And finally, 'Effort' – it has been noted that if you add workload to an individual's plate but fail to take anything off, there is a high likelihood that the new item will fall off. Even a slight (10%) increase in work beyond existing responsibilities can drastically reduce the chances of the initiative succeeding.

7.5 Conclusion

The benefits that can be achieved by adopting service oriented concepts and principles are abundant. The primary obstacles will most likely be humans. Organizations must commit to training the teams in the new tools, processes and concepts. They must also acknowledge that this is a large transition and some of the staff will be resistant to any kind of change. However, commitment to a change management program, on-going education, workshops and community efforts all increase the chances of success.

CHAPTER 8

Pulling It Together

Jim Green
Chairman and CEO
Composite Software

8.1 Where To Start

Now that you know a lot about SOA, one of the most frequently asked questions is "Where do I start?" The reason this question is not definitively answered by now is that there is no single answer. Some focus on the development environment, others on the registry or the ESB, or on the organization and processes. Each person will attack the issues from a different perspective, and put different priorities in different areas. Since there is no "cookbook" where the ingredients have to be mixed in a certain order, don't worry too much about the sequence of activities while you learn.

As has been repeatedly pointed out in the book, small implementations can be achieved without many of the technologies and infrastructure products described herein. Get to work and do some things on your own. When you run into limitations, you will then know what to look for in planning larger implementations, product selection, and infrastructure capabilities. Unfortunately, you can't become an expert by reading a book, including this one, so 'go get your hands dirty'.

KEY RECOMMENDATIONS:

- Start anywhere, but start nonetheless.

- Learn and measure as you go.

- Come back to this book whenever you seek a refresher on core principles and key considerations.

8.2 Scope Of Implementation

Implementing a SOA system can be as simple as putting together a couple of services to promote interoperability, or as complex as revamping your entire IT system to replace proprietary technology with an extensible reusable standards. The extent of your efforts is entirely dependent upon your objectives and ambitions. There is no 'minimum threshold' and you are free to implement all or part of this book in the manner that best suits your needs. We have provided a lot of information in these pages. But a common theme across the various chapters is: "Think long term. Start small. Implement incrementally." So use what you want and need now and don't hesitate to implement some now and return to the book later for more.

8.3 How To Measure Success

Remember, the objective of all enterprise computing is to support a business need. Success is therefore measured by your ability to serve your organization's goals. Too frequently, however, focus is placed on short term objectives, such as the time to completion of an individual project. By now you will have recognized that the SOA model is focused on making future work more efficient, beyond the initial project. Therefore, measure success over time. If done correctly, agility, reuse, interoperability, and flexibility will enable ongoing work to be done much faster than re-inventing everything for every project.   The long term benefits could be far greater than those garnered from any single endeavor. Your pursuit of SOA could yield long term transformational benefits to your organization. It is a worthy cause. We wish you the best of success.

8.4 Summary Of Recommendations

In our attempts to help, many suggestions and recommendations have been made throughout the book. As a final reminder, the key ones have been collected together for your convenience, as follows:

Chapter 1: Getting It Right

- Don't let anyone overwhelm you by trying to teach you everything at once.
- Do as much as you can digest, learn from it, and then add to it.
- Regardless of the distance you travel, have confidence that you are on the right path.
- SOA is the only good alternative for building large scale systems.

Chapter 2: Designing Services

- Base your services on vendor independent industry standards to ensure the best reuse and interoperability.
- Create and deploy your services in an appropriate and best-of-breed infrastructure to ensure operational efficiencies (e.g. an information server for data services; an application server for transaction services.)
- Design service interfaces that are simple, consistent, well documented, and motivated by business requirements to ensure adoption, reusability, and expandability.
- Employ security policies to meet the business needs of your enterprise.

Chapter 3: Registries and Repositories

- Recognize the importance of documenting and maintaining a formal System of Record (SoR) of your services, their revisions, and their service level agreements (SLA).
- Understand the difference between a Service Registry and a Service Repository.
- Put a SoR in place for control and visibility before you need it.

- Reconcile your use of a SOA SoR with your existing Software Development Lifecycle Control (SDLC) system.
- Go further than just acquiring a Registry and Repository system. Plan how you are going to use and maintain it.

Chapter 4: Enterprise Service Buses

- Develop a solid understanding of the capabilities and limitations of the basic web services request/reply protocols versus the enhanced capabilities of an ESB.
- Analyze your interoperability issues and determine whether you will need an ESB to reconcile incompatibilities.
- Understand the different kinds of ESBs and which would be best for you.
- Think through what "role" you want an ESB to play in your system.
- Decide what forms of "mediation" you want from your ESB.

Chapter 5: Runtime Management

- Understand the composition and behavior of your service network.
- Control your service network as well as detecting, diagnosing and, ultimately, preventing problems that arise during the operation of the service network.
- Ensure the correctness of your operational system as it evolves over time.

Chapter 6: Organizing for Success

- Establish and enforce architectural standards and guidelines.
- Set up and empower centralized groups to enforce governance and evolve them as needed.
- Recruit and/or train personnel with the appropriate skill sets.
- Leverage an effective capacity-planning mechanism.
- Create an appropriate funding model.
- Draw up well-defined guidelines for identifying, modeling, implementing, discovering, consuming, and deploying services.
- Implement a portfolio of service-management capabilities.
- Align your software development lifecycle (SDLC) processes with your SOA efforts.

Chapter 7: Capability Development

- Start with a skills assessment of where you are today.
- Develop a training roadmap that integrates with your SOA strategy.
- Tailor training by role to maximize individual and organizational effectiveness.
- Tailor the training to your environment.
- Leverage training providers to accelerate adoption.
- Complement training with change management to ensure new skills are utilized.

Chapter 8: Pulling It Together

- Start anywhere, but start nonetheless.
- Learn and measure as you go.
- Come back to this book whenever you seek a refresher on core principles and key considerations.

ABOUT THE AUTHORS

David Besemer
Chief Technology Officer
Composite Software

David joined Composite in 2002 as VP of Engineering and then transitioned to the CTO role in January 2006. At Composite David pioneered industry-first information server products for high performance query optimization and SOA data services. He joined Composite from his freelance CTO consulting practice where he provided software technology intelligence to venture capital firms. Previously, David served as CTO of eStyle, ran a successful enterprise software consulting practice, headed software product marketing at NeXT Computer, built program trading systems on Wall Street, and researched natural language processing systems at GE's Corporate R&D center. David holds a BS in Computer Science from Michigan State University and a MS in Computer Science from Rensselaer Polytechnic Institute.

Paul Butterworth
Chief Technology Officer
AmberPoint

Paul is the Chief Technology Officer for AmberPoint, the leading provider of SOA management solutions. In recognition for his work at AmberPoint, Paul was named one of InfoWorld's Top 25 CTOs for 2007. Prior to founding AmberPoint, Paul was the CTO for Forte Tools at Sun where he was voted a Distinguished Engineer by his peers and was responsible for the technical strategy for the Sun developer tools products. As a co-founder of Forte Software, Paul was the Chief Architect and Senior Vice President of Engineering and Customer Services. Before founding Forte, Paul served as Chief Architect and Director of Product Engineering at Ingres Corporation. He holds both a BS and a MS in Information and Computer Science from University of California at Irvine.

Luc Clément

Co-Chairman

OASIS UDDI Specification Technical Committee

Luc, an industry expert in UDDI standards, served as Co-Chair of OASIS UDDI Specification Technical Committee from 2003 to 2007. In this role, he oversaw development of all UDDI registry-related specifications, personally editing and co-authoring the OASIS UDDI Version 2 and 3 specifications and Technical Notes, which have been a major catalyst for broad enterprise adoption of SOA. Luc currently serves as the Senior Director of Product Management at Active Endpoints. At Systinet and HP from 2004 through 2007, Luc was actively involved in the development and marketing of the Systinet Registry and SOA Governance products. Before that Luc established Microsoft's UDDI Services and the UDDI Business Registry offerings. A graduate of the Royal Military College of Canada, Luc was an Officer in the Canadian Forces for over 13 years.

Jim Green

Chairman and CEO

Composite Software

Jim, a noted enterprise computing technology visionary and roll-up-the-sleeves entrepreneur, guides Composite Software strategy and operations. Prior to Composite, Jim served as webMethods' CTO, Executive Vice President of Product Development, and Board of Directors member. Jim was CEO and co-founder of Active Software, where he grew the company from a start-up to an industry leader in Enterprise Application Integration (EAI) software. During his seven year tenure at Sun Microsystems, Jim led the development of the Common Object Request Broker Architecture (CORBA) specification, the industry standard for distributed objects. In previous companies, he achieved several industry firsts by developing networking and distributed computing products. Jim holds both a MS in Industrial Engineering and a MS in Computer Science.

Hemant Ramachandra

Managing Director, Business Systems Integration

BearingPoint

Hemant is a Managing Director at BearingPoint and a senior leader responsible for strategy, sales, development and delivery of Technology Integration solutions. He has more than 17 years experience and has led several information systems strategy, architecture and integration projects in a variety of industries ranging from life sciences to the communication and media sector. Hemant specializes in service oriented architecture, business process management and enterprise search. His technology focus has included SAP NetWeaver Process Integration, Information Builders, and Search technologies. Hemant holds a BS in Computer Science from New Jersey Institute of Technology. He is a frequent speaker and has authored several articles on technology integration, service oriented architecture and the impact of technology on the enterprise.

Jeff Schneider
Chief Executive Officer
MomentumSI

Jeff founded MomentumSI, a leading enterprise SOA consulting firm, in 1997, and serves as its CEO and Chairman. As CEO, Jeff aligns the strategic goals of the company with those of the customers. A hands-on CEO, Jeff spends significant time working directly with clients and keeps a close eye on disruptive technologies and paradigms. Prior to founding MomentumSI, Jeff started his career at 3M working on supply chain and manufacturing systems. In 1996, he wrote the first book on Enterprise Java and continues to write for leading technology publications. A frequent speaker related to emerging technologies, Jeff's concepts of service networks, enterprise vocabularies and the "service oriented enterprise" serve as a blueprint for companies to upgrade not only their enterprise architecture, but also their people and processes.

Hub Vandervoort
Chief Technology Officer
Progress Software

Hub is Chief Technology Officer of Progress Software. As CTO, Hub is responsible for incorporating market and customer requirements into the industry leading Progress® Sonic ESB® Product Family and evangelizing Progress' leading-edge developments in the ESB and service-oriented architecture (SOA) infrastructure market. Hub previously held the position of vice president of strategic services for the Sonic division. Over the last four years, he has built up a highly successful technical services group to enable Progress customers and partners to achieve rapid results with Progress technology. Hub has over twenty years experience as an entrepreneur, consultant and senior technology executive in the networking, communications software and Internet industries. Prior to joining Progress, Hub co-founded and managed several successful start-up ventures.